Our Last Great Illusion

A Radical Psychoanalytic Critique
of Therapy Culture

Rob Weatherill

ia

IMPRINT ACADEMIC

Published in the UK by Imprint Academic
PO Box 200, Exeter EX5 5YX, UK

Published in the USA by Imprint Academic
Philosophy Documentation Center
PO Box 7147, Charlottesville, VA 22906-7147, USA

ISBN 0 907845 959

A CIP catalogue record for this book is available from the
British Library and US Library of Congress

Contents

Acknowledgements

I would like to acknowledge the generous bursary kindly awarded by the academic committee of the Milltown Institute of Theology and Philosophy in Dublin, Ireland, for the completion of this project. I should also like to thank Dr. Cormac Gallagher for permission to quote from his privately circulated translation of the seminars of Jacques Lacan. Thanks are also due to many colleagues and friends, both within and outside the psychoanalytic movement here and abroad, although, I should stress that the views expressed here are mine. These include David Berman, Dick Cameron, Aisling Campbell, Felicity Casserly, Nessa Childers, Aiden Coleman, Anne Coughlan, Margaret Coughlan, Olga Cox-Cameron, Martin Daly, Michelo Delmonte, Coleman Duggan, Mitch Elliott, Barbara Fitzgerald, Michael Fitzgerald, Gordon Fletcher, Kirsty Hall, Mark Hartmann, Dervilla Henry, Elizabeth Holmes, Anthony Holmes, Tony Hughes, Liz Larragy, Rik Loose, Patricia McCarthy, Tom McGrath, Abigail Moran, Michael Moran, Brendan Murphy, Maeve Nolan, Helen Sheehan, Ann Scott, Ross Skelton, Patricia Stewart, Rupert Strong, Helena Texier, Robert Young and many others, whose names, for reasons of confidentiality, I cannot include here. I am also grateful to David van Buren for his careful proofreading.

Some of the material in this book is based on work published over the last ten years. Chapter One is a modified version of my thesis submitted for an MSc in Psychotherapy, entitled, 'Psychoanalysis and the therapeutic universe.' The first part of Chapter Two was presented to a clinical meeting of the Irish Forum for Psychoanalytic Psychotherapy in December 1993 and subsequently published as 'Black flowers: psychoanalysis and evil' in the *Journal of the Irish Forum for Psychoanalytic Psychotherapy*, Vol. 4, No 1, pp. 33–47, 1994. The later part of this chapter formed the basis of a paper given at an Association for Psychoanalytic Psychotherapy in Ireland conference in November 2002, 'Psychoanalysis and the Night' later published in *The Letter*, No 24, pp. 99–110. Chapter Three is a more developed version of a paper presented originally at a conference in Belfast on the future of the family: *The Family – a Vision for the Twenty-first Century*, on 25–26 March 1997, in Belfast. Also part of this chapter first appeared as 'Smooth Operators', Chapter Seven in *Living Together*, edited by Neill Small and David Kennard, published by Quartet Books, London, January 1997.

Preface

... just as terror, and abjection that is its doublet, must be excluded from the regime of the community, so it must be sustained and assumed, singularly, in writing as its condition. – Lyotard (1993), p. 210

Therapy may be mad. Here, therapy means particularly psychotherapy and counselling, but can be taken to signify the whole therapeutic culture of well-being, with which the West currently covers its nihilism. Therapy boasts honesty, truth and reconciliation in every area of life from the personal, to the institutional, to the multinational corporation, to democracy itself. More and more people believe in therapy because they have lost belief in everything else. For a long time now it has been punching above its weight, caught in a delirium of empathic rooting-out of oppression, clearing the field for its own mopping-up operation, its own peace-keeping role – the postmodern universal ideology of rights and empowerment.

Can psychoanalysis, as distinct from therapy, claim to be different? Psychoanalysis, as an extended description of human subjectivity, is not a therapy, as such, but an encounter with what *moves* people and what constitutes the *truth of desire*. It comes from a contemplative or reflective tradition. It is also an interpretive discourse: at one earlier time an imperialist metalanguage interpreting literature, art and culture; at another, subject to deconstruction itself. The key notion here is the unconscious,[1] which destabilises *any* ideological position. However, psychoanalysis no longer escapes irony. Particularly, the irony that psychoanalysis, in recent times, has done much to weaken the *autonomous* subject and indirectly accelerate the end of Western hegemony in the world. This process is now far advanced.

However, irony tends to be lost in the serious business of being therapeutic. It becomes very difficult to write about *loss*, the subject matter of psychoanalysis, in a world that only celebrates *more*, more of everything, that advocates continual positivity and entertainment, where silence is impossible and depression endemic.

Therapy culture has an answer for *every* human need. This is precisely our problem: how to write about *another* reality, which now is completely unclearly defined, which is perhaps an impossible limit point that *escapes* therapeutic concern and therefore, in a sense, does not even exist! This book is a small collection of essays that attempt to refute, challenge and contest, this widespread belief in integrative goodness and tranquilisation through gratification, personal, technological and political. Not only do these soft strategies *not* touch *the* problem of, let us say, the *inhuman*, but may yet be a cynical distraction, creating delusions of hope. Notwithstanding, solutions proliferate in the free market, to the precise degree that there may be *no* solutions. In this respect, the therapeutic world view is our last great illusion. Therapy is our last reservoir of meaning, the transcendental sign under which we all live and to which we evermore desperately cling.

These themes are taken up in the chapters, which follow. They can be read in any order and some repetition is inescapable. Broadly, however, Chapter One takes on therapeutic ideology and the promise of universal growth. Chapter Two asks the question about the *ethical* responsibility of the subject unknowingly *de*-centred by the death drive. Chapter Three concerns the family, relationships and the rights of the child. Finally, Chapter Four looks at the postmodern situation in the light of the great instabilities created by exponential global consumption.

Notes

1. As the unconscious is the pivotal concern of psychoanalytic/cultural theorising, the reader may be helped by tentatively identifying a number of possible overlapping meanings in our relationship to this meta-concept.
   (1) The unconscious does not exist, or if it does, it is either harmless or it can be effortlessly integrated with the conscious to maintain health. Therapy culture generally privileges this take on the unconscious as do the natural sciences and modern liberal democracies. The subject is autonomous and rational, yet needs empowering. Nothing need be secret; transparency is the ideal.
   (2) In the Name-of-the-Father, the level of the monotheistic religions and psychoanalysis. The subject is split and contradictory, barred by repression. Here, the unconscious is the discourse of Otherness, foreign, secret and uncanny.
   (3) The unconscious as the other of textual deconstructions: psychoanalytic theory in the academy where the text has many meanings *other* to what was intended by the author.
   (4) In the Name-of-the-Mother, dancing *with* the Shadow, Pagan New Age spirituality, the unconscious as celebratory release and creativity and 21st Century therapy. Here the unconscious is *our friend*.
   (5) The unconscious as *radically* Other, the death drive, irreconcilability: *fatal* strategies (Baudrillard) and ethics (Levinas).

Chapter 1

Psychoanalysis, Psychotherapy & Simulation

Life in-sists before it ex-ists in signs

The power of representation has been grossly over-estimated. In truth, all the power of life lies with life itself. The West is coming increasingly to this impasse, to the inadequacy of representation. The proof of this is that more and more is marketed, imaged, talked through, interacted, as if life can simply be exchanged — talked down, talked out or talked over. A point of meaning saturation has been reached, a vast excess of communication, as if the Real was being forced into the open, being forced to speak and commercialise itself.

Our questions are these. Can what now passes for human reality exclude the Real[1] completely? Is reality now reduced and transmuted into a simple yet universal *therapeutic* version of itself? Is this new sentimental order a ruinous cover for Western apathy and apeasement?

Each element in the world must promote its therapeutic value. From individual (psycho)therapies to large corporations: all missions must be therapeutic. Caring, like Vodafone's 'How are you?' or BT's 'It's good to talk.' Everyone must share, or be helped to share through therapy, what MacIntyre calls an 'emotivist view' of the world, 'freed on the one hand from social bonds of those constraining hierarchies . . . and on the other hand from what modernity has taken to be the superstitions of teleology' (MacIntyre, 1981, p. 34). Flotation and negotiation make up our public and private worlds, marking the end of strong institutions (constraining hierarchies) like, for instance, marriage, the church, politics, schools. We have achieved what Philip Rieff coined as the title of his well-known work, *The Triumph of the Therapeutic.*[2]

Therapeutic culture gratifies every need *before it is articulated*. Far from creating a lack (Lacan), a transitional space (Winnicott), or a renunciation of drive (Freud), it creates a voracious appetite for deconversion which demands its therapeutic products and services minutely researched and differentiated, creating a free-fall and the desublimating effects of continuous gratification and change. A devotional regime for the self is the new ascetic.

Things are fated to disappear into their own sign systems. The real has been replaced by *signs* of itself. On all fronts and on all channels the Real is being forcefully promoted. Yet, individuals experience new radical forms of helplessness on at least three levels. Firstly, an eerie sense of a loss of values, once held in awe, the ground on which mankind has traditionally taken its bearings. Secondly, a suppressed impotence, often disguised as competence, in face of the endless multiplicity, hierarchy and overwhelming reproduction of signs. Thirdly, *no people*, only digital functions, automated machines, electronic barriers, dispensers, prostheses, etc. Into this expanding void comes therapy. Therapy, care, support, help — the comfort zone of the postmodern.

The Excess of Sharing and Caring

One no longer just goes for help. Instead, one enters a whole ideology of caring. Just as one no longer shops, one enters a whole lifestyle promotion, in which *you must know how to play your part*.

Therapy for every possible condition: seductive, soft, warm, supportive, suggestive, hypnotic, congenial, client centred. We can heal your inner child. Get in touch with your true feelings. Co-dependent? Co-dependent no more. This course will identify and clarify co-dependent behaviours and enable you to let go of unhealthy and stressful behaviours. Lovingly seduced into better functioning, better shape, good form. Is this the essence of therapy today? A vast Americanisation of life and a commercialisation of human aspirations — *all the signs of health*.

Been abused as a child? The group will offer you an opportunity to explore your own issues — in relation to self, your body and to others. Or, looking at issues affecting how women see themselves, the aim will be to empower women, to increase our self-worth, and to overcome shyness about our own bodies. Remember: your body is beautiful. Focus on your own healing process. The group offers a safe place to explore memories. Use your power to improve relationships.

Experiment with new and more satisfying ways of relating. Learn to befriend fear and learn what it has to teach us about ourselves.

There is no aspect of modern life not catered for by some therapy product. Several hundred types of therapy exist, perhaps more. All are now becoming accredited, professionally organised, marketed, niche marketed. Undoubtedly, therapy has come to fill the place vacated by traditional religions, but, much more importantly, the place left by the end of the social. Just as commitment to friendship, fellowship and conviviality was being lost, there came an explosion of 'Public Relations', agencies for the commercial promotion, management and exploitation of relationships at every level in every cultural sphere. On all fronts, the destruction of personal ties and direct conversation with the other, in favour of the aggressive promotion of these through publications, glossy literature, videos and the internet, to 'demonstrate our commitment and sincerity'. In short, the *therapeutic relationship* was born.

There is multiple artifice. Firstly invention, then re-inventions wholly at the cost of the Real. The notion of an 'original' seems hopelessly nostalgic and irrelevant. Instead, the Real has become careless, expendable. Like so much household waste it is destined for recycling. With the disappearance of the referent comes a new liberation for signs and what Jameson designates as 'floating signifiers'. Messages can circulate without friction with the Real, and the burden of having to mean anything in particular, except themselves. This makes possible circular banalities: explanations at the simplest level and the seduction into multiple beliefs — this breathing method, this posture, this crystal, this mantra, this fashion, and so on. The uncommitted mind can believe anything. Here is the problem: how to teach people *not* to believe.

Believe signs, consume signs, but forget people. Increasingly the *human* becomes redundant. Objectified 'functionality' is all that is required for therapeutic efficiency, like those robotic arms that mimic human movements in car assembly lines. For instance, the communication function is insured by electronic interactivity; the political function manipulated by the media; the sexual function guaranteed by *in vitro* technologies and internet sex — the safest sex; the critical function maintained by indifference; the criminal function underscored by crime management and conflict resolution techniques.

With the growth and promotion of public relations, there has been a parallel growth of its sister pathology: *paranoid relations*. Mutual antagonism, suspicion and litigation haunt the devastated sites of the social: harassment, victimisation, abuse, bullying, unfair dismissal, miscarriages of all sorts.[3] With that, precautions, safeguards, security systems, documentation of intimate detail, recording, monitoring, all under the imminent threat from the other who can turn from a friend and colleague to an enemy, according to the instantaneous logic of imaginary relations. Screens to watch over us, at work, at leisure, in the precinct, in the car, the *caring* gaze.

As ordinary devotion was disappearing, Rogers developed the perfect version — 'unconditional love', which is the unconditional mimesis of love. When the real drama of life waned and with that the possibilities of identification with substantial figures, we invented 'psychodrama' and 'role-playing'. As the family weakened, 'family reconstruction' and more particularly 'family therapy' became the therapeutic focus, to monitor and manage the breakdown. The erotic was eclipsed and replaced by sexual rationality, the explosion of sexual therapies, sexual technology, sex education and the joy of sex. And so on and on with fabrication after fabrication, reinventions, make-over after make-over, relentless change.

With the creeping feminisation of the West came the demonisation of male psychology as 'inherently violent'. Feminism is the engine of therapeutic logic. Up until recently, male virtues were held in some esteem, but with the second phase of the longest (and the softest) revolution, came a plethora of workshops, conferences, etc., aimed at *reconstructing* men, facilitating men 'to negotiate change and personal development'. We aim at 'healing' the male psyche. Gathering men too help them express their vulnerability, bringing them in from their position on the outside. The loving embrace will lead men into the intra-uterine environment of total hospitality and generosity. Central to this embrace is the deconstruction of heretofore positive notions of masculinity.

The therapeutic work to be done on men world-wide, under the auspices of the UN, involves, for instance, the active promotion of homosexuality, the assertion that men are the cause of (domestic) violence, the elimination of all traditional forms of masculinity from the coming generations. Masculinity is a 'social construct' that is learned and can be unlearned. The net effect has been the leveling out of difference and the attempted therapeutic neutralisation of sexual tension. (An older notion that there might be something ineffable and enigmatic about the Other sex is dismissed as dangerous patriarchal mystification.) Instead, the signs must float (here as elsewhere) between the genders without restriction in the free sexual market.

Even time itself, the very registration of the passing of the Real, has undergone its own chronic revolution, whereby rhythms that tied us to the Real of the world have been overpowered and rendered anachronistic. During the 1980s sleep became impossible with 24-hour markets, news and entertainment. This marked the end of circadian rhythms and the beginning of a generalised insomnia — an unbearable wakefulness in the heart of the darkness of the night. Around this time chronic-fatigue-syndrome was invented to designate symptomatic states of exhaustion in a world unable to rest and sleep, tormented by day-round consumption. Even the birds, at least in urban areas, began to sing by night as well as day.

A brief history of time. (1) Agrarian time governed by the cyclical nature of the seasons and religious festivals. (2) Production time eliminated agrarian time, being governed by the serial mass productive *artificial* rhythms of the eight-hour day and the negotiated time of the working week, holidays, etc. Finally, (3) consumption time and the end of all rhythms and punctuations and the beginning of total flexibility in global time. These radical new a-rhythmias destroy all *real* connections forcing the creation of virtual ones — electronic and therapeutic. Just as Harrison's mechanical chronometer coincided with production time, this final phase of consumption time coincided with the development of the atomic clock (as early as 1945) with an accuracy of one in ten billion. The loss of the Real of time passing created an obsession with measuring it ever more accurately. The most modern clocks achieve an accuracy of 1 in 10^{15}. Such accuracy makes possible global positioning technologies. As with time, the wholesale loss of our bearings, our place and orientation, can be made good via the virtuality of GPS. The precision real will give us our time and place, even though these have lost any real meaning.

Same Games

Professional therapists and professional clients — deep artifice. One creates the other in a closed system of signs and conventions.[4] Each knows the game so well, by now. Therapy for therapy's sake. 'I'm working on myself', a young therapist says. But how can you work on yourself? The same working on the same? But there is no need for a reason. Freed from the need to signify anything, therapy develops its own utopias. Therapy is therapy — identical to itself. There is no distinction between therapist and client. In one (manic) paradigm, there is no longer any sickness. We are *all well*, except that some of us have not achieved our full potential. That is, there is no such thing as illness. Or, in another opposite (depressive) paradigm, we are *all sick*, 'normality' is neurotic, even psychotic. Both paradigms indicate the need for therapy! These ideologies are being circulated at a time, when from a certain practical point of view, the Real of sickness and distress creates an increasing social hierarchy and differentiation. Therapy, however, occupies a parallel (para)sympathetic universe, timeless and sublime, in awe of its own absurd and apparently limitless possibilities.

There is no tradition, religious or secular, that cannot be stripped of its contextual gravity, that is its *absolute otherness* to the contemporary, and be exploited by the ruthless eclectic imperialism of modern therapy. Myth, music, dance, painting, Buddhism, Taoism, Christianity all purloined, and made to work in the service of self-expression and true communication. These integral forms, traditions, are melted down, so that they can be marketed for weekend workshops to 'free creativity' or 'to get more in harmony with yourself'.

Consider *holotropism* (whole growth), for example. It boasts various shamanistic procedures, aboriginal healing ceremonies, the healing trance dance of the King bushman and other groups, rites of passage, psychedelic therapy, certain forms of hypnosis, other experiential psychotherapies, different spiritual practices including controlled breathing, music and other forms of sound technology, and focused bodywork.

One up-market psychotherapy institute advertises its training. The glossy pages of its prospectus are interspersed with *bons mots* in ancient script format from, for instance, Kierkegaard, St Augustine, C.G. Jung, the Talmud, Kant, Nietzsche, Emerson — all of whose thinking is reduced to the same vapid spiritual slogans. For instance, 'One must have chaos within one to give birth to a dancing star' (Nietzsche). 'The greatest loss, that of oneself, may pass unnoticed' (Kierkegaard). All thought is made holy and manipulated to address the alleged narcissistic wounds of consumers:

> Beauty will grow inside us, we will flower, what is asleep will awaken within us, the majesty of the soul, the dreamer of dreams, the little child will sing, you will become a Radiant Warrior, soar to electrifying heights, Ascension, Chanting, Universal Consciousness ...

Another example, from a different source:

> Our course director is a business management consultant specialising in change and innovation. He also uses myth, ritual, dance and storytelling in his work with the world's largest multinationals in a new way of using complexity and transition ...

Business, therapy, myth, complexity, chaos — all these terms have become equivalent in some vast anamorphosis. However, the terms in this mix, even now, are not equal. The multinational ethos absorbs the others, dissolving difference, leaving no trace. At one time business and therapy were opposed. That seems a long time ago. With hardly time for metamorphosis, therapy has been killed off and reborn to become part of the global soft-speak of technology itself. Therapy has *become* a multinational and corporations have become therapeutic (caring for you and caring for the environment). Nowadays, to set therapy *against* corporate business might cause some hilarity. However, the irony is lost on these serious practitioners. These innovators, these global therapists need to create the illusion that they are still breaking down barriers, still heroically fighting old boundaries of repression, vertical hierarchies and ignorance — the ignorance of the West. They are 'on our side', the side of the people and human aspiration. Well before the Wall came down in 1989, the barriers of time (across centuries) and space (between continents) were already down, creating infinite cultural dilution. However, it is necessary for these entrepreneurs to continue to create the *appearance* of opposition and difference, to be seen to be fighting shadows where now there is universal light, brought about by the success of the therapeutic itself. Similarly, the Old Left has been reabsorbed, in much the same way as the body has therapeutic substances, antioxidants, that mop up free radicals.

Therapy continually re-invents itself. The copies become copies, and so on. Yet each mutant form proposes itself as the avant-garde. With each new gloss comes an incremental rise in entropy, as in all forms of copying the later images become degraded. Therapy has faded to the point where it becomes indistinguishable from the general background noise, which, in its turn, has become generally but weakly therapeutic.

It is no longer possible to be critical of therapy and therapy culture because there is no *outside* in which to distance oneself. Psychoanalysts used to say: if you criticise our theory, it is only because you're resisting (you haven't had [enough] analysis).[5] Your critical position was undermined but not impossible. Now, it is more serious. If you are *not* in therapy you *must* have a problem. If you feel critical of therapy, well there is help for that too. Work on your resistance.

Art is therapeutic, as is writing, crying, economics, prayer, flower arranging, sport, sex, education, laughter and so on. If David Lodge said tourism is wearing out the planet, then, we suggest, therapy has worn away the soul; it is the laxative for the soul's prophylactic expulsion. By making everything speak without reserve, therapy is evil.

Mastery

The inexorable logic of mastery. Not content with dominating the natural world, the West turned its attention inwards and aiming at mastery of self, mastery of signifiers and affect, the identity of the Same. 'You can control your thoughts; you can control your feelings.' Work on the self. Historically, there is movement from horse power to steam power to electrical power to post-industrial 'self-power'. Human relations *training* and communication *skills* are notions that would have sent a chill through an earlier generation, enchanted by the Real of imperfection and averse to objectification in all forms. But now, after mass production comes mass seduction, all the way as far as cold seduction — seduction not by people, but by chilled therapeutic systems. The *singularity*, which is the human subject, is generalised potentially to all objective levels of complexity and cybernetic control. Training and regulation will bring about 'healthy functioning'. This mastery is the flexible mastery of the light touch and soft-speak that promotes itself as natural, fluid and cyclical — the therapeutic end point to which history is moving. Visible phallic mastery has changed into its invisible seductive form, against which there can be no resistance. Far from it, we *insist* on the therapeutic controls lovingly bestowed upon us. Here the natural will finally yield itself, open itself, to the caress of therapeutic transparency.

However, Freud spoke about the navel of the dream, which can never be interpreted and which never transpires.

> There is often a passage in even the most thoroughly interpreted dream which has to be left obscure ... at that point there is a tangle of dream-thoughts which cannot be unravelled. ... This is the dream's navel, the spot where it reaches down into the unknown (Freud, 1900, p. 525).

Incorrectly, there is hope that 'layers' of the unconscious continue to exist in secret, without being forced into psychotherapeutic circulation. Does the navel represent a counter-mastery of symbolic absence, an anti-enlightenment strategy, part of the dark matter of the universe? To think in essentialist terms (layers, matter, etc.) is to put structure on absence. But at some point there is resistance to the worldwide work of therapy. Derrida summarises Freud's five forms of resistance, and concludes that the death drive and the repetition compulsion are *the* resistances *par excellence*, the hyperbolic resistance, the irreducible resistance and 'the one that disorganises the very principle, the constitutive idea of psychoanalysis as analysis of resistances' (Derrida, 1996, p. 22). Paradoxically, Derrida goes on to speculate that the desire to analyse, indeed, the 'psychoanalytic theory, treatment, and institution represent the death drive or the repetition compulsion *at work*' (p. 24). So the greatest resistance (the death drive) also disguises itself as *non*-resistance, via its relentless therapeutic rigour, as the very motor of the therapeutic age, to make the world transparent and meaningful. It is the progressive spirit of the times, openness, accessibility, visibility itself, and the only thing it does not analyse is itself. As Derrida says, it is the resistance *of* analysis.

Explosive Imagery

All is surface, reflections in tinted glass, with no solid real upon which to call. The real is another mirage of slippage which, as you get closer and closer, tends to disappear. Instead, there are endless reproductions and refractions, or 'spectaculars'. Globalised mediation of the Real has lead to an explosion in the imaginary, sucking in, liquidating the carefully differentiated Symbolic, Imaginary and Real into an all-embracing term — the *hyperreal*. This is the aggravated real, the media's pre-emptive strike on the world. In short, the reality principle has been replaced by the certainty principle.

Life continues in its simulated form as heritage. Even very recent history is simulated. Coal mines have become museums. Villages become heritage centres. In East Germany, it is possible to be arrested by the secret police, and be interrogated and tortured in a Stasi prison.

In Ireland, we name new buildings, shopping malls, housing developments, etc., after the historic houses they have destroyed. Destroy a woodland and call the subsequent housing development 'Holmwood'. Market the whole country of Ireland for its open green expanses (the Emerald Isle), brought about by the death and emigration of vast numbers of the rural poor during the famine of the 1840s. In the West of Ireland you can take part in organised 'famine walks'. One day the *real* victims might suddenly return from the ditches and hedges to join our over-weight friends in shell suits and trainers weighed down by camcorders and guide-books.

As the truth of any narrative of the subject has become highly subjective, problematic, unstable and ungraspable, *re*-present it, promote it, package it — a *personal* heritage series — the themes of which are cast in stylised and ideological forms: child abuse; child of alcoholic parent; child of divorced parents; child of violent father; child of a re-ordered family; survivor of satanic abuse, alien-abduction, and so on. These people *know* what their problem is. They will queue to humiliate themselves on daytime TV to prove it.

At a stroke, eliminated, the complex interweaving of a history. Currently, hypnotherapists and the primal analysts, manipulators of the so-called 'true/false memory syndrome', (your problem was your parents abused you), have eclipsed, cut across, and finally laid to rest that whole problematic that Freud wrestled with, namely *Nachtraglichkeit* (deferred action) and infantile amnesia which belongs to the 'prehistoric period' between the ages of one and three, 'the same period which is the source of the unconscious and alone contains the aetiology of all the psychoneuroses' (Masson, 1985, p. 302). Freud again writes to Fliess, 'it is a question in the first instance of a *gap in the psyche*' (p. 169), between the lived event and its registration in the mind. In a letter nearly a year later, Freud again, 'As you know I am working on the assumption that our psychic mechanism has come into being by a process of stratification: the . . . memory traces being subjected from time to time to a rearrangement in accordance with fresh circumstances — to a retranscription' (p. 208). Freud speaks here of a number of registrations, perhaps three, corresponding to successive epochs of life. At the boundary between two such epochs a translation of the psychic material must take place. Repression is a failure of translation. 'Thus', he says, 'an anachronism persists: in a particular province, *fueros* are still in force; we are in the presence of "survivals"' (p. 208). These *re*transcriptions, *re*tracings, *re*groupings of traces, survivals and so on, indicate that memory is complex, fragile and unreliable, the very opposite of a video library.

The notion of screen memories implies that memory is fictional, secondary and derivative. That means that every presentation of an alleged original memory is always already a re-presentation, a screen version. Freud concludes, 'Memories *relating* to our childhood may be all we possess' (Freud, 1899, p. 321).

The screen is all there is. The *lived* life across time (diachrony) is radically dissimulated in a synchrony, a now, a theme, a homogeny, a totality. As Levinas states: '[T]hings turn into time and consciousness, independently of the soundless space in which they seem to unfold in a mute world' (Levinas, 1981, p. 35). '[B]eing leaves the night for an inextinguishable insomnia of consciousness' (p. 30). The way that Levinas theorises the gap, the lapse, the aporia, 'before' the re-call, the echo which is the ego hearing itself for the first time, should be contrasted with the current *violence* of spectacular hyperreality.

Forcing: '*Your* problem? *You* were sexually abused'. A few words to encapsulate it all now: 'I was abused. There is nothing more to say. This is my history and if you dare to think anything else you are re-traumatising me. You dare to question my reality.' This is video history — a total image, perfection, complete, marketable, ready for selling, my right to sell it, and everyone buys it. There is no secret here to be uncovered, no childhood enigma, no family, no origin. It is cold hyperreality, clear as crystal, an unambiguous sign — anti-innocence, anti- reticence.

Paradoxically, the mimetics of the Real are so perfect (e.g., electronic music, special effects, computer enhanced imagery, etc.), so sharp, accurate and exhaustively worked on, that the Real's death can only shine through. As is well known, once uncertainty begins to disappear, death is imminent. For instance, regular periodicity, as shown on an ECG, precedes a heart attack. Or a moving dot on a TV screen does not appear to be alive (real) unless a degree of unpredictability is incorporated into its movement. However, even this introduced lifelike unpredictability, like the current fashion for 'naturally aged surfaces' or 'distressed kitchens', remains artificial. Just when the Real appears, it only does so as one more promotional trick.

In the current climate, no horror story is too extravagant. Recovered 'memories' abound, as if they can be simply retrieved from some archaic hard disc of the mind. Take, for instance, satanic-ritual abuse and alien abduction. Alien abduction is real! It is not so much that we are being used by extra-terrestrials for experimentation, who place implants in us in secrecy, but clearly quite the reverse. To the evacuated human subject, the artificial world itself has become alien and abductive. The world has become an alien implant and the global experiment is on. But no one will listen to the survivors.

Similarly, satanic ritual abuse, with its apocalyptic scenes of torture, cannibalism, blood sacrifices, rituals, black magic, has happened. No one believes it! The (black) magic of technology, the continuous ritual therapeutic devouring of the soul is the norm, yet no one believes it. The transvaluation of all values is so complete that it becomes invisible, demonic, the satanic death drive. And like all victims we are collectively caught in the *jouissance* of our seduction: we want more and more to be the mere playthings of some satanic info-techno-media cult, this strange phenomenon that grips the world.

The normal has become paranormal. Our old way of typifying the modern subject as 'narcissistic' or 'schizophrenic' is outmoded. The modern subject is best characterised as *extra*-terrestrial. We have taken leave of our senses. In order to flee from the enormity of the violation perpetrated against him, the subject has not so much become shallow, selfish or fragmented, but instead has quite simply disappeared into another universe. Hence the widespread belief, indeed our last hope, that we might be saved by *benign* life forms from distant planets. We search in desperation for signs of life *out there*, knowing in advance that all life has ceased on earth — only a ghostly travesty of it remains. When our 'news', travelling outwards at the speed of light, reaches those distant solar systems with intelligent life forms, they could be forgiven for believing that the original source approximated to advanced, exciting and intelligent life, unaware the source itself long ago expanded into a red giant, then collapsed into the burnt-out cinder of a white dwarf.

These elaborate stories of abduction and violation are more than just 'hystories' (Showalter, 1997) and 'mimetic disorders' for the expression of inner pain. This is merely to psychologise or pathologise a much more intractable problem, namely the pain involved in the wholesale loss of the world. Now that anything is believable, everything is possible. With no 'quilting-points' (*point-de-capitons*), the Real, for its part, remains easy, cool, indifferent and accidental. But for its criminal lack of regard for us, it must be forced to signify. The real must speak. Increasingly, it can only speak its pain.

Firstly, everyone must be listened to; secondly, everyone must be believed (the illusion of therapy and democracy). Everyone will listen to and believe everyone; this will heal all our divisions. At the same time: no one will listen to anyone; no one will believe anything any longer. In the nightmare we try to shout out in terror but no sound comes out of our mouths. Paralysis grips us.

The universe is therapeutic.

Transparent, Serious and Global Clients

Psychotherapy has created a culture where clients take themselves and their needs very seriously; for so long emotional needs were appallingly stifled by patriarchal repression and authoritarianism, negating personal freedom. Now, *we* have to take responsibility for our lives, for every decision, not only personally, but globally. Personally: no smoking, low cholesterol, stress management programmes and the whole gamut of personal bio-feedback, psi-feedback controls, via implanted computer chips, down to the level of sexual and genetic expression. Globally: you are responsible for waste, pollution, for deforestation, global warming, for racism, for sexism, and so on.[6]

Remembering THE EARTH:

> A workshop of ancestral, evolutionary, and ecological rituals and practices, designed to restore our awareness and our memory of our interrelations with the sacred earth. Drawing on Shamanistic traditions from different parts of the world, on ancient European animistic mythology, and on insights from ecology and evolution, we will focus on reconnecting with the spiritual intelligences inherent in the natural world.[7]

Try to remember yourself. Be good to yourself and the earth.

Radically individualised, each atom is not only answerable to itself, but the whole environment. This is the burden, the labour of liberation. One is expected to be ethically pure in a cosmic dimension, and at the other extreme, need-oriented and emotionally pure and gratified in the subjective dimension.

A new infantilism is invoked — a dramatisation and escalation of demand which must be satisfied, increasingly at the level of the body itself. Self-esteem is the key measure. The over-exposed simulated self is also hyper-vulnerable to slights. Militantly mindful of needs and human rights to happiness, suffering becomes intolerable. The elimination of suffering world-wide is *demanded* through therapeutic agencies, down to animal and plant liberation.

In the absence of children in areas of affluence, adults are making up for this sudden and alarming disappearance by becoming children themselves, with childish demands. New lifestyles, built with new money, mean that increasingly we separate when a *real* child (i.e., not perfect, not the imaginary child) enters our mutually gratifying exotic relationships. Unable to bear this much reality, either children are forced into hot-housed simulations of ideal children, or we disband, leaving the children to be the grown-ups and endure the real suffering that we are forever unable to face. Therapy demands that we all become little children and be gratified and healed. What it didn't bargain for was a new *lethal* and incurable form of childhood — the new infantilism — screaming for needs to be heard and respected.

Micro-Simulations

As biology students in the 1960s, we were always reading about 'HeLa cells' in the scientific literature. These cells were used in molecular biological laboratories all over the world to determine the ultra-structure of cellular components and processes. It turned out that HeLa cells were cancer cells, taken from a patient, whose name, it was revealed, was Henrietta Lacks. She died of cervical cancer in 1951, aged thirty-one. Her cells were the first human cells to be grown outside the body. For half a century after her death, these cells have been propagated in laboratories around the world. Only the name given to these cells retained some trace of their history. Hardly anyone knew Henrietta Lacks, but a riotous portion of her, these disordered cells, was cloned and transmitted all over the world. Her cells are now available in frozen whole cell pellet form, cryopreserved, ready-to-use proliferating cultures. Self-renewing cells that have no need of an origin, replicating themselves into eternity. These 'human' products are marketed in 'sexy' ways in scientific journals. Likewise, at some critical point in the past the social body became sick. Violent proliferations of the social (techno-info-mediated communication) sprung up everywhere as this body was dying. The death went unnoticed and metastatic forms of the social took over and multiplied uncontrollably in an artificial world.

Synthetic ethology is the study of animal behaviour in a synthetic world. More broadly, artificial life is defined as 'a field of study devoted to understanding life by attempting to abstract the fundamental dynamic principles underlying biological phenomena and recreating these dynamics in other physical media — such as computers — making them accessible to new kinds of experimental manipulation and testing' (Langton, 1997). Computer generated life forms, behaviours, communication and evolution available on screen. As the need for the referent does not arise *ab initio*, this is the purest form of simulation offering a therapeutic utopia. The mind is a biocomputer or the computer is a mind (AI), it makes no difference, as all drift towards the artificial and interactive, parodying or copying themselves and each other *without end*.

These 'forms' are immortal; there is no 'soma' as such to die. Like the HeLa cells they have given up death and sexuality. Like Weissman's protista (see Freud, 1920, section 6), current asexual reproductive cloning techniques, stem cell research, cryogenics, the trend is towards the repetition compulsion, de- differentiation, i.e., the propagation of the Same in artificial media, metastasis, the death drive.

The Care of Ruin

Modern counselling and therapy came of age in the 1960s. It has hardened up into a growth industry that has expanded beyond all expectations and projections. Therapy has no natural predators. It has its critics, but they are no match for the whole sentimental ideology that devours all values, all difference, as it joins hands and sends hugs across every former frontier, every former domain of otherness. People are queuing to get in on the act. Just as it is said everyone has a book in them, everyone must have a therapeutic self.

At every major disaster, the counsellors compete with the media, getting in the way of the paramedics trying to help victims. In March 1994, a twelve year-old schoolgirl was murdered in her classroom by a crazed gunman, in Middlesborough. Immediately a hotline was set up for counselling. It was announced that the next day there would be counsellors for every class in the school, together with educational psychologists and social workers.

Membership of the British Association for Counselling and Psychotherapy (BACP) stands at 16,000 compared to 1,300 in 1977. Apparently, 9,000 therapists offered their services to New Yorkers following the September 11th disaster in 2001. George Bonanno, from New York's Columbia University said the counselling was 'an enormous waste of money . . . there is more data supporting the view that talking about how unhappy you are just makes it worse.'[8]

There will be a free helpline after the show. Our lines will be open, and there will be trained counsellors on hand to listen to your problems. Do call. Help is always at hand. There is now a massive health industry that feeds off the decay and detritus created by the system itself. Economic benefits, the vast new opportunities for saprophytic growth created by the breakdown of the social — dislocation, crime, addiction, violence, trafficking, etc., are enormous and growing (see for instance Hitchens, 2003). Distress creates economic activity — huge investments in new training programmes, government bodies setting targets, educational strategies, health packages, counselling courses, web-sites, electronic products for stress management, phone-ins, marathons, the mass mobilisation of help by the caring society, which above all, likes to see the spectacle everywhere promoted of its caring ethos.[9] Every screen, every commentator creates images of care which is the culture's symbolic debt to the destruction of the social.

The liberal elites have secured their lives in face of the anxiety of continuous change and uncertainty. They understand the nature of the modern calamity, know all about the breakdown of the social — after all, they were the first to advocate 'liberalisation' and the first to experience its benefits.[10] Hence the importance to the middle classes of the relationships that can be controlled, underwritten and guaranteed, like the relationship with the professional therapist. The elite in every modern state propagates the illusion of well-being and equality via therapeutic strategies of pretence and 'political correctness', across all media. Goodness is forced to accumulate all on the one side, while the black political and libidinal economies are free to proliferate in some parallel register, which, like the dark matter of the universe, present everywhere but unseen, holds everything together.

The Death of Therapy

Therapy is hyperventilating to enter the Real of emotional life. Intoxicated with power, therapy proliferates with new forms, new mutant strains to meet explosive demands in hyperreality. What will be the life cycle of this caring phenomenon? Will its universe expand further and then implode into a mass death, destroyed by overheating — sexual indiscretions, abuses of power, abuse of traditions, religions, art forms, ecology, abuse of every secret? Will the Real rise up and avenge itself on such loving omnipotence, on obscene coherence, perfection, knowing and working out and over of everything? Or, will it die in its own trivialisations, clichés, promises, its white-washing of the Real?

However, lest this account plays into the hands of the numerous critics of psychotherapy, all the way from Eynsenck, who claimed that recovery rates in psychotherapy are no better than chance, to Crews, who claimed that Freud was a charlatan, let there be no mistake, therapy and counselling do work. They work well, and many patients are the better for undergoing them. On the level of the image, or the 'borrowed mask of being', therapy is bound to work, linked as it is to some *distant* humanity, however debased, functionalised and sentimentalised this has become.

Therapy never leaves us alone, this is bad enough, but psychiatry, psychopharmacology and neuroscience *occlude our very existence*. Here, smart therapies are fine-tuned at the level of molecular and biochemical modulation. For psychiatry, both personal history and subjectivity never existed. Science forecloses the subject. The mental or the biological machine is nothing more or less than a complex biochemical expression and unfolding of the code. Intervention at the level of the mind in psychotherapy is one thing, but intervention at the level of the synapse and optimal mood regulation, in spite of the whole anti-psychiatry movement, dominates the field by far in the competition for *normal simulations* of mental health. Objectification, reification, here is the system operating at the highest level.

A television programme on anorexia nervosa refers only to abnormal levels of key hormones produced by the hypothalamus in the victims. After a hundred years of psychoanalytic research, no mention is made of the anorexic's terror in face of her oral sadism. More broadly, a BBC Radio Four programme (13/3/99) on the well known F.R. Leavis debate between the arts and sciences, stressed the 'mechanical' nature of science as well as the 'beauty' of its discoveries, etc. Lamenting the relative lack of enthusiasm for the sciences in Britain, *no* speaker referred its terroristic elision of subjectivity. While scientific metaphors are deployed in the arts, it never works the other way around. We should not be alarmed: *the subject has no place in science.*[11] Likewise, therapy works best when we are not there, allowing it to approach its own ideal, its own superfunctioning. Scientific therapies are exemplary: there is no excuse for dysfunctioning, barring side-effects. In the absence of the human subject, any remaining obstacles to the therapeutic world order are finally overcome. This is the secret aim of all therapy — to work toward our own disappearance. At present, as we have demonstrated, we are no more than a support, a cause of therapeutic desire. If we slipped away, nothing would change! Or, has therapeutic success *without opposition* created its own negative therapeutic reaction out of its own collective unconscious sense of guilt, whereby its 'crime' of the elimination (of clients) must, by a symbolic equivalence, be followed by its own implosion?

Can anything stop this death drive?

Psychoanalysis and the Symbolic

Psychoanalysis was the prototype from which all other forms of psychotherapy and counselling have evolved and adaptively radiated to reach every corner of contemporary life. Freud's modernist reductions of religion set the pace for the triumph of the order of imaginary emptyings and the destruction of illusion. His was one of the starting points for what has become a global industry of psychological sloganising, and transgressive re-illusionment. Can psychoanalysis itself escape its own analysis and its own outcomes? Is psychoanalysis not guilty, at least, by association, of being in the wrong place at the wrong time, i.e., being the catalyst that speeded up the breakdown? Or as one critic put it, 'of being the disease of which it is itself the cure?'

Insofar as psychoanalysis is still obscurely and secretly connected to a religious domain (a secular religion, Nina Coltart), a *symbolic* domain, it may escape some of this opprobrium of success accorded to therapy. To the extent that psychoanalysis remains a vocation, not a profession, it might still have the freedom to do its work, i.e., to contemplate loss, malediction, begin the burden of mourning. In this sense, psychoanalysis is the *opposite* of therapy. It categorically renounces force and empowerment.

Religions have been professionalised as well, and have to take their place in the market (tele-evangelists), and in liberal culture (the ordination of women), but the symbolic ritual gravity of religion, inasmuch as it still exists here and there, creates a difference.[12] In general though, religions have gone the way of psychotherapies. *There is no other logic*, religions must become therapeutic and therapies must become religious. Therapies are the trend-setters for religions, by their multiplicity, their endless joviality and triviality. Religion and psychotherapy must be fun — the games people play!

When my mother was dying of cancer and had given up (in terror) all hope and had stopped speaking, I found myself reading parts of the Bible to her, although she had no religious belief or practice. At other times we would sit for long times in silence. The symbolic has an effect. Words that have authority. One can still do something in the face of death.

The symbolic is the domain of the pact, the gift of sacrifice, of obligation, of ceremony and ritual, of a secret brutality (the wrath of God) and formalised and significant marking (castration). Baudrillard says the symbolic haunts modern social institutions in the form of their own deferred death.[13]

In the very close-knit structure of the criminal Kray gang in London, the Kray henchmen feared the legendary brutality of the twins themselves. But all felt relieved and *proud* to have been cut — cut with a knife for a mistake or a deception. They displayed their scars, on their faces, on their necks or arms — evidence for the fact that they had been marked or punished, and were therefore part of this great organisation. They had been initiated and they had to carry the marks of castration to belong.[14]

A man injured his leg badly in a motorcycle accident. The doctors thought of amputating it, but decided in the end that they could save it. They did so, but the leg was deformed. In order to bring about a *real* amputation, this man laid his leg across a railway line in a very careful manner so that a train sliced it off cleanly. In another case report, a man wanted to disable himself. He had the overwhelming desire to cause one of his legs to be amputated. No doctor obliged him with an operation. In desperation, and with elaborate precautions, he fired a gun shot at a precise distance from his leg. He then tied the tourniquet. Covered in blood, he phoned for an ambulance. Relief, the amputation *was* necessary. No doubt, extreme and pathological as these examples are, do they not demonstrate the desire for a *real suffering*? Therapy culture sees to it that we lack nothing, there *is* an 'other of the other', the world is complete in its synthetic happiness: forcing the only thing left — the return to a sacrificial logic.

Baudrillard speaks of the symbolic, 'as a functioning principle that is sovereignly external and antagonistic to our economic "reality-principle"' (Poster, 1988, p. 120). However, he warns:

> If we start yearning nostalgically, especially these days, for a revitalised 'symbolic order', we should have no illusions. Such an order once existed, but it was composed of ferocious hierarchies; the transparency of signs goes hand in hand with their cruelty. . . . Caste societies, feudal or archaic, were cruel societies (p. 136).

The archaic was brutal, whereas the postmodern is therapeutic. The archaic has been systematically exorcised by the progressive extension of scientific reason to eliminate disease via 'magic bullets' and smart drugs, discontent via hyper-consumerism, creating perfect scenarios which fail to have written into them their own death. Death and suffering, systematically (even holistically) forced out of the picture, will accumulate on the Other side, in the anarchic domain of the Baudrillardian symbolic.

Freud developed his death drive theory at that moment when, following the carnage of the Somme, the radical illusion that death might finally be eliminated by scientific reason and human perfectibility, was exploded. The Symbolic demands that life cannot survive *unilaterally*, accumulate all goodness to itself. The Symbolic demands that *death circulates* in a system of total reversibility and exchange which is excessive, orgiastic and sacrificial. The Symbolic puts an end to the games of repression, differentiation, rationality and semiocracy.

Consequently, the exorcism of terror and suffering and the administration of happiness, meaning and gratification become the system's own death drive. By continuously improving reality, exposing all illusions, of being therapeutic on a global scale ('We care; we care that you care; we are caring for you!'), an abyss opens up of radical disenchantment and disaffection, exploding into violent imagery as the absolute screen against death. This subtle therapeutically controlled freedom becomes terroristic. True to the symbolic rule, the therapeutic becomes its own pathology: the disease for which it itself continues to believe therapy is the only cure.

One French TV station actually managed to capture on video a motorway pile-up in fog in which more than ten people died. You could see the cars, lorries and coaches pile into each other slowly and silently, in an almost careless image of the ice-cold real. The camcorder was shaking a little. Overall, this has little effect though, it was just a news clip. *Nothing stops the traffic.* In a matter of hours, there will be nothing left, a trace only, a skid mark, splinters of glass perhaps. Real, hyperreal, who cares? Keep moving. Don't stop. Keep cool. Nothing can *arrest* us anymore. The modern consumer travels 15,000 miles a year! Back and forth in our metallic sarcophagi, but where to, for what? Road deaths, the modern form of sacrificial logic — violent, meaningless, excessive.

Against the spectral presence of symbolic exchange, the *forcing* of everything: of the erotic in pornography; of communication in therapy; of value through the commercial code; of history through heritage; of the event through the spectacle; of the sport of politics and the politics of sport, scoring every time. Everywhere, life enforcement and life enhancement, living on borrowed time, fearing the final diagnosis. Suffering has been forced into the vast recycling system called therapy. Therapy is heating up the planet, creating devastating storms in the social, changes that are probably irreversible. Holes appear everywhere at a rate that exceeds the system's repair mechanisms to close them over.

Breaking Presence . . . Smithereens

Does anything *tear through* the simulation, the text, the speech? Jameson suggests that: 'the stereotype [the simulation] is what is already preconsumed, aesthetically prepared for consumption, whereas the palpable struggle to get sense data into sentences leaves a residue in its failure, lets you *sense the presence of the referent* outside

the closed door' (Jameson, 1991, p. 150). It is to these residues of failure, where the image falters, speech staggers, where the interminable talking might stop and attention might minimally be paid. This is
the notion of the sublime, what is *un*-representable and beyond.

The texture of the paint in the picture, the timbre of a musical
instrument, the *saying* of the voice in the said, the epiphany of the
face, the irremissibility of suffering, are all occurrences, happenings,
the sublime, that occurs 'before' any commentary. No doubt they all
enter the circulation of indifference and the 'it happens' will become
yet another discourse — the diachrony saved but lost in being saved
in the synchrony of explanations. The mute world, as it were, forced
into speech for our clients who are probably yawning, exhausted by
the surfeit of meanings.

However, Lyotard refers to an old treatise, Dogen's Shobogenzo,
the Zenki where he speaks of 'a breaking presence which is never
inscribed or memorable'. Instead, 'There can be a presence that the
mirror cannot reflect, *but that breaks it to smithereens*' (Lyotard, 1988a,
p. 55). Into discourse comes this 'breaking presence'. For
Baudrillard, symbolic exchange, later, seduction and all manner of
viral terroristic forms, that might have the fatal power to subvert the
tyranny of the code. For Freud, the death drive. For Plato, Agathon.
For Levinas, the ethical relation.

From this perspective, therapy is better understood as 'a dialogue
of the deaf', to use Lyotard's phrase. Therapy is deaf to this tearing
through or the breaking presence. We might be thankful for that failure to hear, the inaudibility of the Real, against the frenetic protesta-
tions of care coming from customer care departments, whose every
promotional urge is minutely researched, market tested, monitored
and packaged to bolster the last illusion — that we really care, we
care for YOU. If the Real so much as makes the briefest appearance,
its sublime secret, its presentness to itself, will be taken, betrayed
and above all made to work — not the work of mourning, loss and
disappearance, but *forced* appearance and selling.

What is never stressed is the ego's *primary* exposure to Being,
without prehension or comprehension. In Draft K to Fliess, already
referred to, Freud states that, 'Hysteria necessarily presupposes a
primary [my italics] experience of unpleasure . . . of a passive nature.
. . . This first stage may be described as 'fright hysteria'; its primary
symptom is the manifestation of fright' (Masson, 1985, p. 169). The
notion of an 'overwhelming' (*Uberwaltigung*) of the ego is present
throughout Freud's writings (e.g. Freud, 1893–95, p. 263; 1937, pp.
234ff; 1939, p. 78), where it forms the basis for all neurosis. When
referring to paranoia, also in Draft K, Freud speaks of the so-called
'assimilatory delusions' as 'the beginnings of an *alteration in the ego*,

an expression of its having been overwhelmed.'[15] In Section V of *The Ego and the Id*, Freud states that, 'What it is that the ego fears from the external world and from the libidinal danger cannot be specified; we know that the fear is of being overwhelmed or annihilated, but it cannot be grasped analytically' (Freud, 1923, p. 57). That is it *cannot be represented*. In *Inhibitions Symptoms and Anxiety*, Freud refers to 'traumatic situation', which entails helplessness in the face of an accumulation of excitation. This is the 'quantitative factor'.

Back to the beginning of Freud's work, and the mystery of Q, 'which possesses all the characteristics of quantity (though we have no means of measuring it [representing it]), which is capable of increase, diminution, displacement and discharge' (Freud, 1894, p. 60). At the beginning of the *Project*, Freud raises the whole problem of Q (from the external world — exogenous) and Qn (endogenous stimuli) in relation to 'neuronal inertia' and the 'endeavour at least [of the mental apparatus] to keep the Qn as low as possible, to keep it constant' (Freud, 1895, p. 297). When this control of Q fails, pain is experienced: 'pain consists in the *irruption of large Qs into w* [impermeable neurones] . . . [T]here is no obstacle to its conduction' (p. 307). Freud likens this to a strike of lightning upon the system. In Chapter 4 of *Beyond the Pleasure Principle*, Freud refers to the 'living vesicle', 'suspended in the middle of an external world charged with the most powerful energies' (Freud, 1920, p. 27). A protective shield enables the 'sampling' of the external world, but 'towards the inside there can be no such shield' (p. 29), and from this Freud derives the origin of the primitive mechanism of defence, termed projection, from which we get the whole confusion between inner and outer. The breaking through of the protective shield results in pain. This represents a trauma and results in an 'anticathexis' on a grand scale to bring about 'binding'. Failure of this binding process leads to the *beyond* of the pleasure-reality principle, resulting in the more primitive, 'demonic' Repetition Compulsion and the ultimate conservatism of the Death Drive and the lure of the inorganic.

In phenomenological terms,[16] unable to *grasp* what life is, the subject is affected (with quantity!) without the source of affection ever becoming the theme of representation, meaning or analysis, accused or condemned in face of the Real *before* being able to assume an identity. To use a Levinas metaphor, we are too tight in our skins, burst open by an excess, thrown into life, placed in a perilous and inescapable position, without any consolation, orphaned and exiled *before* belonging, familiarity and recognition, already irradiated and expelled from the world as we come into it.

In the very hypostasis of the subject, there is, what Levinas terms a 'a null-site', a breathlessness of the spirit, a break-up of essence.

Humanity is the 'excluded middle', between being and non-being. Excluded from everywhere. Subjectivity is the locus of this non-identity, the saying out of breath, in which the diachronic past cannot be recuperated by memory or history, is incommensurable with the present (an essence or totality that begins and ends), subjectivity becomes an 'unassumable passivity'. As Levinas says, '"*Se passer*" — to come to pass — is for us a precious expression in which the *self* (*se*) figures as in the past that bypasses itself, as in ageing without "active synthesis"' (Levinas, 1981, p. 14).

Kundera, in a recent work of fiction, captures something of this *se passer*. 'The more vast the amount of time we've left behind us, the more irresistible is the voice calling us to return to it. . . . Men grow old, the end draws near, each moment becomes more and more valuable' (Kundera, 2002, p. 77). In his story a man and a woman meet by chance while returning to Prague, their homeland, after twenty years, when they chose to become exiles from communism. After such a long exile, picking up the threads of their brief love story, their memories no longer coincide:

> [M]emory retains no more than a millionth, a hundred-millionth, in short an utterly infinitesimal bit of a lived life. . . . For after all, what can memory actually do, the poor thing? . . . We won't understand a thing about human life if we persist in avoiding the most obvious fact: that a reality no longer is what it was when it was: it cannot be reconstructed (p. 123).

Being overflows. The subject is an exception and ex-pulsion in its responsibility, subject to everything, the ego is struck, cut across, awakened from its imperialist dream. Against any therapeutic notions of empowerment, Levinas stresses: 'The self is a *sub-jectum*; it is under the weight of the universe, responsible for everything' (Levinas, 1981, p. 116). In an inescapable state of awareness, without potential limit, Levinas formulates his ethics: 'It is through the condition of being hostage that there can be in the world pity, compassion . . . the little there is, even the simple "After you, sir"' (p. 117).

Awareness and responsibility depend upon the opposite of the atomising processes of postmodernity. Against dispersion, separation, Levinas proposes an already constituted 'proximity'. 'Proximity is fraternity before essence and before death' (p. 139). Fraternity, being my brother's keeper, precedes, is the foundation for, is the pre-emptive strike on any promotional globalisation, any mission statements about togetherness. For Levinas:

> The unity of the human race is in fact posterior to fraternity. Proximity is a difference, a non-coinciding, an arrhythmia in time, a

diachrony refractory to thematisation. The unnarratable other loses his face as a neighbour in narration (p. 166).

Humanism, like therapy its commercial offspring, has to be denounced only because it is not sufficiently human. The world weighs with all its suffering and all its fault on the ego because this ego is a *free* consciousness, capable of sympathy and compassion. Freedom with no time to assume it, unfree to slip away.[17] Ethics is outside: 'It signifies outside of all finality and every system' (p. 135). The possibility of origin and progression is shaken entirely by our being captured and ordered as, *hostage* to the other, substituting one-self for the other, 'a responsibility ordered for the first one on the scene, a responsibility for the neighbour, inspired by the other, I, the same, am torn up from my beginning in myself, my equality with myself' (p. 144). Ethics is the break-up of the originary unity of tran-scendental apperception, witnessed but not thematised, by 'a sub-ject supporting everything, subject to everything, that is, suffering for everyone . . . ' (p. 148). For Levinas, the locus of this suffering is the *face* of the other in its naked fleshiness prior to its entry into the world.

> The face of the other is not straightaway representation or the pres-ence of a figure. . . . Before the countenance the face adopts or assumes (and through which it enters the system of the world and is perceived, grasped and possessed, comprehended and appre-hended within that system as a means of identification), it is sur-prised in its nakedness, destitution, and uprightness of a defenceless exposure to death (Levinas, 2001, p. 253).

Levinas often quotes Dostoyevsky: 'Each of us is guilty before everyone and for everyone, and I more than the others.'[18]

In time, everything is sclerosised into therapeutic substance, with nothing to lose, except the lapse, which does not return and there-fore we might tentatively forget it. Being thus appears like a game, without responsibility, a betrayal, an apology for being. Essence, identity is ironical and a cover for anxiety about Being. Identity is a de-facing of the face, like an old building covered over by graffiti. Therapists are those well meaning souls that supply the 'children' with the spray cans to destroy the old doors and walls, etc. Essence has no exits; therapy has seen to that. From essence comes comedy, tragedy and eschatological consolations.

The ambush of the ego by (the quantity, the excess of) life itself constitutes the lethal background radiation of global therapeutic systems, whose repair mechanisms are wholly inadequate to the task set. Therapy can never talk down this real of catastrophe, the breaking presence, the nakedness of the Face, against which it pits everything including its credibility. Trauma, too great to be taken up, *prior to* any traumatic event as such, is the softening up process before the Real of the world. Here therapy ducks out. And why not? Because to be caught in the anarchic glare of Being would mean becoming overwhelmed to the point of total passivity.[19] Therapy, therefore, becomes unreceptive, unresponsive, indeed *unaffected* by life itself. Cynically, coldly and with no nonsense, it severs its connection with life and joins the system, becoming the system itself. Professional therapy is cool. This is its lie which lies at the base of all its imperialist pretentiousness. Therapy stands accused of two elisions: (1) the failure to avow traumatic passivity in face of the total proximity of being that overflows itself beyond every container — our being at the mercy of being, prior to all memory, freedom and representation. (2) Promoting the desecration of all the bars (the law, repression, etc.) that would shield us from the full glare of the light, from which there is now no protection except the pathetic illusion of more and more therapy, to try and borrow some 'mask of being'.

Once therapy ceased to be a vocation it lost everything. A vocation is a calling, a call from the Other. We are called *before* we have any freedom to respond. The call precedes any essence or capacity of the 'I'. It holds us hostage in a black universe. A vocation implies a receptivity to the Other beyond any limit. The response comes to *encounter* the call which is without words — the silent cry of the Other, the prayer uttered in solitude or agony, which marks the absolute separation of the infinite from the finite. A vocation is the possibility of a hospitality and a welcome that exceeds itself, becomes a hostage without substitution, in its radical passivity towards Being.

Notes

1. The Real is the most elusive of the three Lacanian 'registers', the Symbolic, the Imaginary and the Real. The Symbolic and the Imaginary make-up *human* reality, while the Real is the unsymbolisable remainder, closer to Being-in-itself, *beyond* appearances. The Real is like the sea: seamless, undifferentiated, infinite, cold and indifferent. The Real is Other (capital 'O'). The impact of the Real is always experienced as a shock because of its *im*-mediacy. The Real is complete in itself; it lacks nothing. It is the unsayable, the unspeakable, the impossible. Much of what follows is a critique of therapy culture's frenetic and exitless artifice in face of the irremissibility of the Real.

2. Rieff was a key figure in asserting that therapy brings about what he termed as 'moral disarmament' and the creation of 'the virtuosi of the self'.

3. The list of abuses seems endless. *The Oxford Dictionary of New Words* documents the various forms involving virtually every relationship. Into the infinite space, distance and freedom that has opened up in what we still quaintly refer to as 'the community', comes a poisonous intimacy, a negative erotic of hate and antipathy. All former relations of trust and reciprocity must now be 'outed' and scrutinised to rate their abusive potential, to make

victim impact assessments. Only *professional* relationships are safe enough, therapeutic enough to engage in. All others are traumatic and therefore should be avoided.

4. Therapies are so well promoted that clients already know how they should 'be themselves' in a given therapy situation. That is, how you might present yourself in, for instance, a psychotherapeutic situation, as opposed to a cosmetic therapy, or alternative therapy, etc. These would all be different but entirely predictable. Clients are even given guidance before they arrive as to what to expect and how to co-operate.

5. Freud's statement is as follows: 'We have been obliged to recognise and express as our conviction that no one has the right to join in a discussion on psychoanalysis who has not had particular experiences which can only be obtained by being analysed oneself' (Freud, 1933a, p. 69).

6. This global responsibility, taken very seriously by the therapy classes, has the reassuring function of returning an ethical sign to the middle class with minimal effort, creating a comforting sense of the emerging global *community* — the edifying spectacle of a network of caring, educated and responsible people like us around the globe. Remember: what *we* do is consume *with care*.

7. From: 'Towards Earth Community International Conference.' Held in Ireland, 1994.

8. See report in *The Sunday Times* (London). March 2, 2003.

9. The reaction to the sudden death of Diana (31.8.97) is a case in point. The nation cried for itself, for the *image* of its first lady and its finest heroine of therapy. Post-imperial Britain had at last gone soft and given in to the tears. Some therapists believed this was our finest hour, when we had come of age as a therapy culture capable of pure subjective absorption and its mirror image through television. Therapists have been encouraging the British to cry for years. Well, this was it: the moving and restorative image of ourselves watching ourselves cry, indeed a millennial spectacle we should be proud of.

10. Liberalisation came in two stages. (1) From the New Left in the 1970s via social legislation freeing up divorce, abortion, gay rights, etc. (2) During the 1980s the New Right brought in economic freedoms and outlawed restrictive practices.

11. We should not be fooled by the postmodern 'inclusion' of the observer/ subject in the new holistic paradigm for science whereby the complexity of, for instance, the neural networks, gives rise to consciousness and subjectivity which can then have a complex feedback effect on the systems that give rise to them. This is no more than the logic of therapy now incorporating science, where the case vignette is used to 'humanise' the scientific explanations of various disorders.

12. January 20, 2002, BBC Radio Four broadcast an Eastern Orthodox service. The service comes from the Northernmost monastery in Russia, Solovki, which the Soviet regime turned into a death camp for Orthodox priests. This place has seen not only generations of pilgrims; after the Revolution of 1917, tragedy struck. There was already a wall, built in the Middle Ages to keep marauders out. Lenin's henchmen threw out the monks and the monastery was ready-made to become a prison camp. The first, it became also one of the worst. Unlike Auschwitz, it was intended primarily for labour rather than extermination, but the effect was not so different. Tens of thousands, the flower of a whole generation of believers, died here, ravaged by disease, starvation and the execution of anyone who stepped out of line. Bishops, clergy, political leaders, the intelligentsia perished here almost

anonymously. Here is a poem written by one of the inmates, during the Soviet times.

We are left to bloom where the King of Souls has sown us. If he has sown us in the field of sorrow, let us bloom in sorrow. If he has sown us in solitude, let us be in solitude, for the Creator sows even the most beautiful of flowers on inaccessible tracks between mountain paths. They have their value, even though nobody sees them. The anguish of the soul is unseen, but like blossoms it can be plucked and offered to the Saviour.

13. Psychoanalysis, almost alone, amongst therapies and popular religions, emphasises an *existential* guilt that is inescapable. Psychoanalysis designates the distinctly un-therapeutic notion of a guilt stemming from Oedipal *wishes* (the phylogenetic trace of the murder of the primal father), prior to any actions that might arouse and justify guilt.

14. Here is a link with the widespread practice of ritualised circumcision, subincision, excision and infibulation, where the cut marks the passage of the initiate from non-existence to *being* within the tribe. The individual needs to be marked by the Symbolic domain. The cut is the mark of 'recognition', the passage from non-being to being, by which initially, at least, The subject is spoken *for*. The ritual cut is celebrated as the entry point into the world. However to a modern sensibility, such practices are barbaric as we have no need and even less understanding of symbolic obligation, the covenant — 'The uncircumcised male who is not circumcised in the flesh of his foreskin, that *he shall be cut off from his people*; he hath broken my covenant' (Genesis xvii: v 14).

15. Freud (1896) p. 227. Masson has it slightly differently as 'the beginning of the alteration of the ego, as a statement of defeat' (Freud in Masson, 1985, p. 168).

16. Here, Freud's mysterious physiologically/psychologically mechanistic 'Q' becomes the immanence of Being or Life.

17. In practice, there has to be a limit state to this infinite responsibility for the other. This is the 'third party', the birth of thought, the Law, Justice and philosophy.

18. I. Turgenev, *Brothers Karamazov*, quoted in Levinas (1981), p. 146.

19. Anarchy here is not the reverse side of order. It must be understood as a radical Other, beyond anything that we have known. It is beyond the dialectic, order/disorder. It is not a playful chaos from which creativity may emerge. On the contrary, anarchy is pure persecution, being cut through, by what Lyotard and Levinas refer to as the in-human, which pays no heed to us. In psychoanalytic terms I have described this as the death drive (see Weatherill, 1998; 1999).

Chapter 2[1]

Black Flowers: Psychoanalysis & Evil

Winnicott often referred to analysis as the adult capacity to play, in a properly subversive sense — play being something that is subversive of the work ethic. Masud Khan spoke of 'waiting', '[w]e cannot talk of waiting without talking of death' (Khan, 1988, p. 188). The silence in the analysis, is the silence of death. This comes closer. Beyond playing and waiting. Bion cautioned analysts not to try to cure people. His ideal of foregoing understanding involves the temporary loss, in some degree, of the analyst's ego, and it makes all the difference to the conduct of an analysis. It means that the analysis remains always open to the possibility of what Bion calls the evolution of 'O', the infinite. The playing theory of analysis can easily become, as we have been stressing throughout, the autoerotism of therapy, implying an essentially circular pleasure, self-centred, a self-caress which includes the other, indeed welcomes the other, providing the other is really the same.

The good, the positive, the happy is part of the new global autoerotic, the world-wide playing with oneself, the climaxing of capitalism. Many religious sects believe in the 'second coming', therapy more modestly believes only in our 'coming into our own, or, 'our coming on our own', the total realisation of pleasure, our getting off on ourselves and our healing.

As for psychoanalysis, one cannot explain it. At the very least, work, progress and productivity in analysis may be hoped for, invested in, increasingly taught and promoted, but all this good healthy therapeutic activity operates in a domain that totally exceeds it. Instead, one *submits* to psychoanalysis. It is a passive process of receiving, opening to the Other. At the back of everything is the 'O', the zero, the Void, always, the limit point, the impossible.

Death Against Life

The relationship between Eros and Thanatos is not symmetrical. There is a radical antagonism on one side — a principle of irreconcilability. Eros is the principle of reconcilability, reconciling good and evil, reconciling love and hate, creating syntheses, our whole earth ethic, but the death drive has another reference. It refuses life in favour of death. Now, cornered, as it were, by the life and the work/play drive of therapy, the death drive becomes ever more virulent. Currently, it is fighting for its life in a wholly positive world, of positive thinking and human rights.

No one believes this dualistic theory for a moment. This is our dilemma. Freud's final drive dualism, radical desire — desire beyond desire — is equivalent to the death drive. In this formulation, sexuality now under the name of Eros is no longer the disruptive force it once was. It is no longer the free spirit of the primary process and the pleasure principle, but has been seduced into quiescence, bound-energy, the reality principle and secondary process activity. Eros has become safe sex. Whereas the death drive, according to Laplanche and Pontalis 'takes over as the "primal", "demonic" force which is of the essence of drive, while sexuality — paradoxically — goes over to the side of the binding process' (Laplanche & Pontalis, 1974, p. 242). Furthermore, they comment that the death drive is 'a reaffirmation of what Freud had always held to be the very essence of the unconscious in its indestructible and unreality aspects. This reassertion of the most radical part of unconscious desire can be correlated with a change in the ultimate function which Freud assigned to sexuality' (pp. 102–3). In fact, Laplanche, in his own right, renames Freud's death drive as the 'sexual death drive' (e.g. in Weatherill, 1999).

There are still some heretics, some *true* believers. Taking Freud further, or what is implied in his final revision of drive theory is precisely this: the death drive consists in the negation of dialectics, a radical dissociation of Good and Evil, and by extension, the *autonomy* of the principle of Evil. The Good presupposes, erroneously as it turns out, a dialectical involvement with Evil. Whereas, Evil is founded on itself alone, in pure incompatibility. Evil is thus master of the game, outside the loop. It is the principle of Evil, the reign of eternal antagonism, that must eventually carry off the victory.

Here is something unknown, unrepresented and unbelievable, what Freud described as *unheimliche*, a strangeness that emerges within the familiar. This is an alterity beyond all other, foreign, seductive, exotic, fascinated with ecstasy and death, with a hidden universe of fatality, the surrender of everything to a *non*-human agency, an agency which is external to the human and delivers us from it. Narcissism protects us from this domain, via therapy as we have been stressing and the whole range of therapeutic strategies available. We are thus serious unbelievers in the death drive.

Beyond narcissism and its whole security apparatus, lies the energy that paradoxically sustains it coming from elsewhere, the parallel world everywhere of antagonistic forces which have nothing to do with a social morality or the law of historical progress. The protective line of narcissism is getting thinner while all these morbid forces gather themselves on the Other side.[2]

These deeper energies are fatal energies, vertiginous, exhilarating, inviting absolute danger and promiscuity. From the vantage point of the good, morality and progress, from the side of humanism, the death drive carries such a negative sign that it doesn't exist, it is simply not credible. Even aggression, its nearest bearly tolerable relative, is something we must 'work' to be 'freed' from through therapeutic strategies and anger management.

Bion reminds us that our lives begin in catastrophe to which we are destined to return, unless we have found a good container along the way. Freud spoke of the primal repression (*Urverdrangung*) of an excess of excitation, and of a permanent anticathexis (e.g. Freud, 1915, p. 181). But the anticathexis only belies the potential greater attraction (enjoyment) of what is primordially turned away from. This catastrophic unconscious nucleus of origin acts like a magnetic pole, a point of fixation, a centre of gravity, pulling us back. The catastrophe is always potentially present, yet the chaos may be slowed down to reasonable proportions — making, as they say, making the chaos work for you. Therapy becomes the management of chaos, the controlled release of enjoyment.

Bion speaks of the primacy, *not* of mind and thinking, but of hallucinosis: 'This state [hallucinosis] I do not regard as an exaggeration of a pathological or even natural condition: I consider it rather to be a state always present, but overlaid by other phenomena, which screen it' (Bion, 1970, p. 36). Hallucinosis has to do with the immediacy of gratification of pleasure and pain, not thought and meaning. 'In the domain of hallucinosis, the mental event is transformed into a sense impression and sense impressions in this domain do not have meaning; they provide pleasure or pain' (p. 37). Bion continues, 'Thinking remains subordinate to the satisfaction of sensuous desires' (p. 121). For Bion, psychoanalysis seems to be a thankless task, an uphill struggle against thoughtlessness.

> The human animal has not ceased to be persecuted by his mind and the thoughts usually associated with it — whatever their origin may be. Therefore I do not expect any psychoanalysis properly done to escape the odium inseparable from the mind. Refuge is sure to be sought in mindlessness, sexualisation, acting-out, and degrees of stupor' (p. 126).

The mind is a bad object threatening to awake us from our pleasurable suffering (dreaming, hallucinating) to which we are inordinately and fatally attracted. The mind threatens with the painful detour of thinking, when in truth all that is wanted is just to live. Hallucinosis is life. Life is hallucinogenic as it toys with speed and catastrophe.

For Kleinians, as we have noted, this speed living, ecstatic living (ex-stasis), is described psycho-theologically as envy. Envy is the inheritance of every *finite* being aware of the infinite. Envy is the closest relative of the death drive, as Bion demonstrates.

> The model for cancerous growth is not splitting of the object but splitting of envy, each 'bit' then growing independently of every other 'bit'. Ostensibly these bits appear as 'different' ideas. In fact they are a cover: ideas — impulses — ONE impulse. In this respect sessions can be regarded as repeating themselves, and the unchanging quality of the sessions should betray itself despite the multitudinous changes in disguise. Sometimes this state is described as a negative therapeutic reaction when it would be more accurately described as 'proliferation of fragmented envy' . . . envy of the personality capable of maturation (Bion, 1970, p. 128).

The delirium of life becomes metastatic. Islands of cells, metastases, give up on the lawful signals dictated by their neighbours, and roam around the psyche-soma with one aim in mind — envious fragmented proliferation. Cancer is mindless growth, the absolute freedom of cells (the right of cells to self-determination) to multiply and vascularise. Tumours appear in different tissues, but with the same aim, the deconstruction of the banality of order, the overthrow of authority, the end of differentiation. The normal metabolic order is subverted with no hope of reconciliation. There is no dialogue with cancer. Cancer is the free market of pure incompatibility, the revenge of the Other of the body.

Bion (1965) indicates how poor human beings are in making use of their thoughts, 'because the capacity to think is rudimentary in all of us' (p. 14). Later, again he says, '"thinking", in the sense of engaging in that activity which is concerned with the use of thoughts, is embryonic even in the adult and has yet to be developed fully by the race' (p. 85). Therefore, the psychotic patient 'seems unable to think or imagine a situation but has to act it out . . . hence the tendency to produce problem situations instead of solving problems' (p. 40).

Transferred to a global scale, time may be running out. 'Learning' has been outstripped by our technological development and our tendency to produce multiple problems. As we approach such technologies as quantum computation, for instance, thinking about them is clearly out of the question. This has been the case for more than one hundred and fifty years — the point at which technological complexity began to exceed ordinary human understanding and therefore human control. Thinking has been clouded by the great benefits technology bestows locally, as it were, missing the point that in its totality it is awesome, inhuman, rendering humanity homeless in ever-increasing numbers. Unable to think about this awesomeness, it may become a *passage a l'act* in a kind of global psychosis, where the maintenance of any kind of control is minimal to say the least. Where, according to a recent survey, it is no longer just religious freaks from obscure sects, that believe that the world might end during this century. Technology becomes a thing of supreme beauty. Technology becomes *das Ding*.[3]

For Lacan, in his seminar on Ethics, there is an equation between *das Ding*, *jouissance*, the *beyond* of the Law, and evil. Desire brings us to the limit where we risk destruction. The death drive is the Law beyond the Law, the Outlaw, which pertains to nature, to human nature, and from which we always try to separate ourselves by what he calls 'the circuit of goods'. Beyond these goods lies a second barrier, that of the aesthetic, the sublime experience of beauty, which hides, shields us from while at the same time intimating, an unbearable truth pointing in the direction of the field of absolute destruction, what Lacan calls 'destruction beyond putrefaction' (Lacan, 1959–60, p. 217).

Illustrations

We could have chosen, the Death Camps, the Gulag, Vietnam, the Khmer Rouge, Bosnia, Kosovo, the Twin Towers, and so on, to illustrate the non-dialectical excesses, the putrefactive destruction of recent times, for which we have no instruments. We would have to develop a new absolute scale of measurement for such inhumanities, which are by common consent beyond anything imaginable. We will present smaller examples, which nevertheless show the same slippage beyond, the same drift towards infinity.

The Suicide

Here is Milan Kundera's strange girl, whom nobody knows, from his book, *Immortality* (1991).

A girl went out on a highway at night and sat down with her back to the oncoming cars. She sat there, her head resting on her knees, and waited for death. The driver of the first car swerved aside at the last moment, and died with his wife and two children. The second car too ended up in the ditch. And the third. Nothing happened to the girl. She got up, walked away and nobody ever found out who she was.

That's how I imagine her, the narrator continues, and I am sure that she sees herself that way, too: as a woman walking through a valley among people who do not hear her. Or another image: she is at the dentist's, sitting in a crowded waiting room; a new patient enters, walks to the couch where she is seated and sits down on her lap; he didn't do it intentionally, he simply saw an empty seat on the couch. These are two images or metaphors that define her. Her longing for suicide was provoked not by something from outside her. It was planted in the very soil of her being, and it grew slowly and unfolded like a black flower. The longing for self-destruction slowly grew until one day she was no longer capable of resisting it. And so the girl's dream of her own death was born. She carried herself through life as something monstrous, something she hated and couldn't get rid of. That's why she longed so much to throw herself away, as one throws away a crumpled piece of paper. She longed to die like a beetle, crushed by a sudden fist (see Kundera, 1991, pp. 280–300).

This girl has *no* name, *no* voice, *no* body and *no* image. She is not part of any circuit of human exchange or community. She is pure desertion. Her suicidal impulse, therefore, cannot be a 'cry for help', for instance, because this implies a place, however tentative, within the symbolic. Her position is one of maximal distance. She is a negative object, a piece of anti-matter in a universe where everything is reversed. Black flowers unfold, and death grows, a chance encounter means risking death. Death as contagion.

The Addict

Drugs have a powerful neurophysiological effect. Experimentally animals can become addicted, there may be genes that predispose to addiction, but these pharmacological insights have to be re-written in a cultural context. Psychoanalytically speaking, the psychoactive drug exploits a lacuna that opens up post-Oedipally, especially in relation to the oral drive and the need to 'satisfy the archaic oral longing.'[4] In Lacanian terms, the substance that the addict 'uses' represents the object-a — that little (lost) object in the Real, beyond normality, that transfixes our desire, because its presence removes the lack which is essential to any creative living. The substance short-circuits desire. Referring to the alcoholic, Melman states that '[T]he object is an ideal aspired to as a beyond: another effort, the "one more drink" that calls to the alcoholic' (Melman, 1980, pp. 239–40). Melman adds, that on attaining the object the subject disappears, i.e. falls in a torpor, into the gutter. More recently, Loose sees addiction, not so much as a death drive phenomenon, but an attempt to triumph over death and more generally to triumph over a lack that feels like death (Loose, 2002).

The addict is structurally speaking a 'remainder' in our culture, flirting with death, promoting himself as immortal; addicts are abject fall-out from the system. Beyond the law, beyond pleasure: dereliction. We observe on a mass scale the increasing impotence and fragility of the law, the helping professions, the social services and indeed the social fabric itself. Addictive substances illustrate just how easily the (Oedipal) law can be subverted. The radical turn is *away* from the Other back to the *jouissance* of the pock-marked body-self. The substance, the abuser, the pusher and the producer become the focus of an illegal network of violence, causing death and misery. There are parts of modern cities that are completely run by drug barons, or indeed whole countries are subverted – the machinery of the state being turned around to fight crime by criminal means.

Gabriel Garcia Marquez documents what he refers to as the 'biblical holocaust [of narcoterrorism] that has been consuming Colombia for more than twenty years' (Marquez, 1998). Four presidential candidates had been assassinated before the 1990 campaign to tackle the drugs problem. Between 1983 and 1991, twenty-six journalists in the Colombian media had been murdered by the drug cartels. In Medellin, the centre of urban terrorism, deaths were running at twenty a day early in 1991. Marquez comments:

> Easy money, a narcotic more harmful than the ill-named 'heroic drugs', was injected into the national culture. The idea prospered: The Law is the greatest obstacle to happiness; it is a waste of time learning to read and write; you can live a better, more secure life as a criminal than as a law-abiding citizen – in short this was the social breakdown typical of all undeclared wars (Marquez, 1998, p. 130).

The drug culture becomes part of a malign ecology and excess that spreads corruption at all levels: '[I]t was almost impossible to articulate a policy for peace that would position the state on the side of the good, and criminal of any stripe on the side of evil' (p. 132). 'Judges and magistrates, whose low salaries were barely enough to live on, but not enough to pay for the education of their children, faced an insoluble dilemma: either they sold themselves to the drug traffickers, or they were killed. The admirable and heartbreaking fact is that many chose death' (pp. 179–80). Marquez describes youth, from the Medellin slum culture, assigned to guard the hostages of narcoterrorism;

The boys common condition was absolute fatalism. They knew they were going to die young, they accepted it, and cared only about living for the moment. They made excuses to themselves for the reprehensible work: it meant helping the family, buying nice clothes, having motorcycles, and ensuring the happiness of their mothers, whom they adored above all else in the world and for whose sakes they were willing to die. . . . Second only to the saints, they worshipped Rohypnol, a tranquilliser that allowed them to commit movie exploits in real life. 'You mix it with beer and get high right away', explained one guard. 'Then someone lends you a good knife and you steal a car and go for a ride. The fun is how scared they look when they hand you the keys.' They despised everything else: politicians, the government, the state, the law, the police, all of society. Life, they said, was shit (pp. 59–60).

The addict corrupts, the addict is the shit that falls out of the holes of the Symbolic. Unlike, the hysteric, the addict shows no disgust at shit and vomit. As Melman says:

Disgust does not function as a barrier; from vomit to excrement, from incest to perjury, from perverse manipulation to investigative sniffing, there is even an *appetite for waste*; and frank intimacy extends to the alcoholic's spontaneous exhibition of himself as such an object (Melman, 1980, p. 239).

The Commune

Friedrichshoff was an anarchist community set up in Austria in 1971 by a small group of young well educated radicals dedicated to the overthrow of Western bourgeois values and the nuclear family. Like many communes of the time, it demanded the creation of a 'sexual paradise' based on the assumption that 'the couple relationship was the root of all evil.'[5] The early phase of the commune involved the participants in actively overturning all the old sexual taboos. This was forcefully promoted via the excessive use of therapy led by the charismatic 'father' of the commune, Otto Muhl, whom everyone apparently worshipped. He became their ideal. Therapy was used in the service of the death drive, where subjectivity is effaced and the individuals become mere sexual instruments of the primal 'father', objects in a cycle of sexual exchange. For Muhl, therapy *began* with sex, and, as he says, 'they even queued up to wipe my arse.' Nobody belonged to anybody. The repression of all barriers gave rise to ferocious sexual hierarchies and serious outbreaks of venereal disease. After some years, the by-now several hundred strong commune ran short of money, and decided to send 'agents' secretly back into the outside world where they found they could make large amounts of money in the burgeoning capitalist centres of Europe during the 1980s. This money was siphoned back into the commune.

Children were born to the commune members, educated in the cult's philosophy, and in due course were obliged to have sex with the adult cult members. At this point the mothers of these children objected, citing Muhl, who in 1991 was sentenced to seven years imprisonment for child sexual abuse. Soon the commune broke down openly, with many leaving to lead ordinary lives in the outside world. Muhl himself, when released from prison, set up another paradise in Portugal with a few loyal members of the commune. The remainder stayed in the original commune complex, setting up their own apartments, living alone or together monogamously, contemplating the past — was it failure? — looking through the old photograph albums of the orgies. One commentator noted, the photos bore a striking resemblance to those pictures of naked bodies in the Nazi death camps.

Clearly, wildly innovative and counter-cultural in the early 1970s (the Austrian government tried to close the commune), some decades later, it raises no more than a jaded glance. Then, this was serious freedom, a commune that eradicates patriarchal bourgeois values, ironically creates a *primal* father. The bar on the monogamous relations creates *compulsory* polygamy. New Right money feeds radical politics, only when sex occurs with children values are re-awakened. The death drive operates here as it has with many cultic radicals of that period, by creating a *negative* ideal — bloated perverts, war criminals in the sexual revolution. Only the good old-fashioned bourgeois law convicted Muhl, but only as a gesture. The contemporary sexual free market creates many safe havens for these sex warlords, like Muhl, whose only crime has been to take therapy culture very seriously. After all, what they followed to the end was none other than the narcissistic imperative — never weaken, never falter, when it is a matter of your own needs, never give ground to your desire. Fuck everything.

The Adolescent

An article in the *New Statesman*, by Angela Philips, suggests 'that fathers are often worse than useless.'[6]

A young adolescent boy is abusive to his mother. He used to be abusive to his father until he left and hasn't been seen since. Now the mother is terrorised by the boy and lives in fear of him. She does the best she can and still worries about him.

She believed in 'bringing up children in freedom', but from the start, he was cold and unresponsive to hugs and cuddles. She had breast-fed him, but he turned away from the breast soon after starting the feed. She would put him down to sleep, and in no time he would be crying again. The only way to pacify him was to put him back to the breast, and the same thing would happen again. She would then get impatient and shove him roughly back into the cot, and they would then both get into an agitated state.

Now, he is abusing her, shouting, threatening, cursing her, occasionally breaking up furniture and breaking windows. He used to wet the bed, soil himself. Now, big, aggressive, macho, walled in against the world, one night, she was going out, he blocked the doorway to stop her going. A friend intervened and he let her go, but ransacked her room. She tries to reason with him, but he ignores her and goes out. In school, he is known as a mad fighter. On one occasion he punched a teacher in the stomach — a teacher who had tried to help him. He picked fights with older boys. He was barred from classes and even rejected by his peers.

Social workers, child psychologists and psychotherapists, counsellors, police liaison officers, priests, many others, tested their empathic and therapeutic skills on him, but he, in reptilian mode, refused any communication. After many more abusive incidents, the school excluded him. He had no qualifications, no training, no preparation for life. He left home too, cursing and gesticulating to his mother as he walked backwards down the short path. For a time he lived on the margins, in sheds, outhouses, waste land and ditches. Then, people lost touch with him. He has disappeared without trace.

The clinic waiting room of a local hospital has a poster: *grow your own dope; plant a man*. One could be forgiven for believing that the feminist left is currently using one gender to destroy another, just like the old hard left used one class to destroy another.

The Guerrilla Fighter

Chasseguet-Smirgel and Grunberger (1976) report attending a psychoanalytic conference, where the case history of a guerrilla fighter was reported. This man had become unable to participate in armed combat following a situation in which he was forced to kill a man. His analysis was being paid for by the revolutionary organisation of which he was a member. During the analysis, the guerrilla stated that he had realised that his motive for being a revolutionary fighter was that he wanted to kill his father, and in the transference, the analyst. Therefore, he could no longer see any point in returning to the war. His analyst concluded that this was a 'defence', and that the patient was using the analysis as a 'refuge' from the reality of class struggle. He made this interpretation to the patient, who then allegedly 'confirmed' the interpretation with a dream. In the dream he was lying on a comfortable couch and was awakened, not by an alarm, but a chant, 'Comrade, the Revolution calls'. He went back to the front to fight.

The Mother

Juliana Mukankwaya, a member of interahamwe (Rwandan, Hutu tribal militia), 35 year-old mother of six, together with other women, rounded up the children of fellow villagers and bludgeoned them to death. We killed too many to count, they said.[7] This act demonstrates better than many what Lacan has always emphasised that language (ethnicity) *marks* the body. This machete wielding ethnic vengeance, makes clear in a very concrete way that culture cuts deep into the body. Lacan says: 'Man does not think with his soul. . . . He thinks as a consequence of the fact that a structure carves up his body' (Lacan, 1974).

The Ethical Subject

A senior Lacanian analyst, Bill Richardson, raised a small storm when he delivered a paper on ethics in psychoanalysis to a small group of Lacanian analysts in Dublin.[8]

Richardson asks two simple questions. (1) While the analyst's desire is necessarily constrained, the patient's or the analysand's desire, by contrast, is free to be developed through speaking, 'how', he asks, 'are other essential ingredients in the analysand's life (for example, the needs, demands, desires, legitimate rights of other subjects — like spouse, children — dependants of any kind) to be factored in as *limits* to the analysand's desire?'[9] (2) Given the fact that the Lacanian subject is so illusive, fading or vanishing, '[h]ow can so fleeting a subject abide long enough to accept responsibility for anything, that is, be an ethical subject at all?' (Richardson, 1998, p. 25).

Was Richardson going back on the central Lacanian axiom of the split subject? Was he reneging on the absolute freedom of the subject, turning his back on the psychoanalytic movement? Richardson's ends his talk: 'Without an accountable subject, there is no ethics, and an ethics of psychoanalysis no more than chimera. The whole enterprise would have to be rethought, then — or call itself something else' (p. 26).

Should Lacanian psychoanalysis (by implication all therapy), be seen as the pursuit of desire for itself, alone: the gold- standard of desire, free from, resistant to, any domination by the other? This is the extreme position, adopted by Lacan to counter the subtle emotional conformity masquarading as freedom that we have noted in therapy culture. Rejecting notions of healing, happiness, health, curing, doing good, the rag-bag of therapeutic goodwill, Lacan recognised the duplicity in desire, i.e., normative intermittent pleasure on the one hand, versus, the excess of pleasure that leads to pain and suffering. The Lacanian analysand is above all *accountable for his life*. Note Lacan's emphasis on the paternal metaphor, the Other, the

Debt, the Symbolic order, symbolic castration, Oedipus, alienation, the destitution of the subject, the enigma of the Real, etc. *Not* the ego, but the subject — barred at every turn. The Lacanian ethic: you should not give ground relative to your desire, but in the Lacanian universe, dominated only by signifiers already pregnant with death, the price of this ethical freedom is high.

The current emphasis on the signifier in psychoanalysis and cultural theory generally, while being correct and irrefutable ('there is no outside of language'), marginalises affectivity,[10] narrowing the field, leaving aside all the great *ethical* issues to do with affect — namely, hate, betrayal, narcissism, conflict, ambivalence, unbinding, anxiety and suffering. In short, psychoanalysis, disengaged, retreats into the university and the institute, whose courses will buy its (text)books creating a tautology, a solipsism that insulates psychoanalysis from the larger cultural and ethical debates.[11] Psychoanalysis is no different here than any other (therapeutic) institution or discipline, in its decathexis of the world and its retreat into relativism and neutrality.

In a wider sense, there are problems for the humanities in general. Firstly, like the emphasis on the signifier, the emphasis on the 'text' has lead to a gulf opening between the textual reality and historical reality, however problematic and indeterminate such a 'reality' may now be. Secondly, like the so-called fleeting or fading subject, the deconstruction of authorship, of identity, has led to a de-coupling of aesthetics and ethics with devastating losses to both. Thirdly, an idealised and complacent notion of Western civilisation persists, derived from the 19th Century — high levels of literacy, freedom, the rule of Law, the advancement of science, material progress, etc., should be seen against the Real of structural poverty, suffering and violence (located at some distance from the university). For these reasons, the humanities have become *inhumane* and are failing before the Night.

Everywhere, the shift is from the real to the virtual, including the growth and promotion of virtual ethics — the ethical *management* of health resources, human resources, the environment, foreign policy, etc. Instead of real engagement, there comes to birth the mission statement, and such phrases as, sustainable development, clean energy, stakeholder dialogue, environmental impact assessment, working together for biodiversity, inclusivity, access, self-development, continual learning, service provision, networking, equality and so on. These are the vacuous words and phrases that serve the global ideal of 'ethics lite'. A mission, the sending out of persons on a political or diplomatic errand, for the spread of a religion. The 'religion', now part of every public body and its promotion, is passionately therapeutic.[12] Preaching their own goodness, they plead to be heard to be caring, cool and, above all, sincere. They become apophantic. Meanwhile the truth becomes permanently deferrable. Truth is put on hold indefinitely, while the black flowers flower and set seed.

Chasseguet-Smirgel and Grunberger *alone* question an 'analysis' paid for by a third world liberation organisation, where an inhibition in killing is seen as a defence, and where the *manifest* content of the dream is used to serve ideological ends — *comrade, the revolution calls!* The other analysts may have consoled themselves with the thought of 'non-interference', the postmodern ideal of democratic indifference — listening to everyone and not judging. But listen comrades, the death drive calls!

Maruja Pachon deVillamizar, an award-winning journalist, kidnapped in November 1990 in Bogota, held in secret, fearing for her life, suddenly fiercely challenges her young crazed guards, in particular one named Barrabas, who would wake her by pressing the barrel of his machine-gun against her head.

'How can you live like this? What do you believe in? Do you have any idea what friendship means? Does the word loyalty mean anything to you?' Only Barrabas stood up to her. 'You rich motherfuckers!' He once shouted. 'Did you really think you'd run things forever? Not anymore, damn it: it's all over!' Maruja, who had been so afraid of him, met the challenge with the same rage. 'You kill your friends, your friends kill you, you all end up killing each other,' she screamed. 'Who can understand you? Find me one person who can say what kind of animals you people are.'

Driven, perhaps, to desperation because he could not kill her, Barrabas smashed his fist into the wall and damaged the bones in his wrist. He bellowed like a savage and burst into tears of fury (see Marquez, 1998, p. 213).

Consider also Coupland's post-apocalyptic vision as he instructs the hapless survivors:

> Everyday for the rest of your lives, all of your living moments are to be spent making others aware of this need — the need to probe and drill and examine and locate the words that take us beyond ourselves . . .
>
> Scrape. Feel. Dig. Believe. Ask.
>
> Ask questions, no *screech* questions aloud . . .
>
> Grind questions into the glass on photocopiers . . .
>
> Ask whatever challenges dead and thoughtless beliefs . . .

You're going to be forever homesick, walking through a cold railway station until the end, whispering strange ideas about existence into the ears of children. Your lives will be tinged with urgency, as though rescuing buried men . . . (Coupland, 1998, pp. 269–70).

Evil has ceased to exist! Reduced to two or three columns in the authoritative *Oxford Companion to Philosophy*, evil is either an illusion, or a necessary part of the good, or merely a privation of goodness; or evil may be needed for the greater good, indeed for heroic actions, that transcend human understanding. Evil has no entry at all in *The Edinburgh Encyclopaedia of Continental Philosophy*. This disbelief in evil is a consequence of contextualisation and diffusion. Nothing is taken seriously enough to be considered as evil. Any assertions like Adorno's well known, 'no poetry after Auschwitz' is criticised because it puts the Holocaust off limits for political discussion. According to Zizek, for instance, the Holocaust then becomes 'impossible to be accounted for in terms of a power struggle' (Zizek, 2000, p. 112). The designation evil, stops, halts, silences. Discussion ceases. Demonisation will follow, then tabloid racism. But Zizek, himself, talks about 'id-evil', skinheads who feel it's good to beat up foreigners *for no reason*. He calls this 'non- functional cruelty', that is cruelty that manages to escape contextualisation, that is motiveless and random.[13]

It was the same equivocation, disbelief in evil, that allowed the Soviet experiment to continue for over seventy years. Martin Amis, in *Koba the Dread*, deals not so much with what was perceived to be evil (like the Holocaust), but with *laughter* that surrounds the Soviet experiment . The sub-title of his book is *Laughter and the Twenty Million*. He quotes Nietzsche: 'A joke is an epigram on the death of a feeling'. If this is the case here, then, Amis says, 'this joke is a massacre' (Amis, 2002, p. 247). When Robert Conquest was asked what he might call *The Great Terror: A Reassessment*, the post-glasnost revision of his 1968 book, he told his publisher: 'How about I Told You So, You Fucking Fools? (p. 10). Conquest says: 'the reality of Stalin's activities was often disbelieved because they seemed to be unbearable . . . *morally and physically inconceivable*' (p. 262, emphasis added).

If evil does *not* exist, being instead a reductionist, simplistic, lazy demonisation of the other, a failure of understanding, an illusion, or, ultimately possibly, for the greater *good*, what are we to make of these statements from two key figures of the revolution? To what Real are they pointing — functional cruelty? Trotsky: 'we must rid ourselves of the Quaker-Papist babble about the sanctity of human life' (p. 253). Lenin: 'Intellectuals are lackeys of capitalism, who think they are the brains of the nation. They are not the brains of the nation. They're its shit' (p. 15).

The third part of his book is called *When We Dead Awaken*. Amis is trying to wake himself from the moral torpor that disables us in the liberal west, with our middle class guilt, our belief that the Soviet system was being slandered by Right-wingers in U.S. and elsewhere, our belief in the brotherhood of man, our contextualisation. Yet, to be shot, to be starved to death by quota — contextualise that.

Under humanism, evil has become the weak force, challenged, exposed and undermined by the relentless pursuit of reason. Like everything else it has changed into its soft form, whereby it might finally, after its illustrious history, be persuaded (no doubt through therapy) to serve the greater good. Evil created the world and then withdrew, not surviving the missionary saturation positivity created by therapy. Welcome to angelic discourse with its gentle disengagement, effortless sublation, appeasement, general reduction of excitation, its Nirvana Principle.

The logic of therapy:

You say a crime was committed against you and your family in X?

Yes.

In your own time, in your own words, can you tell me about the terrible incident(s)?

(Head in hands) Silence. Therapist waits. After repeated attempts . . .

No. I can't speak about such terrible things. *Never. Never.*

Okay. I understand. But when you do feel you can tell us, remember we are here to help and it will help you if you can share with us what happened.

No. I can't speak. I can only hate those fucking animals, those murdering bastards . . .

Sadly, so our therapist from the troubled area concludes, speaking, almost whispering, as it were, behind the back of his hand:

Here you see all the splitting processes, denial, regression, primary process thinking, engendered by such painful experiences. I'm afraid conflict resolution is a slow process. He *will* speak, most of them do, but it takes time. Much wise nodding of heads amongst the therapists present.

But our aim must be to close this painful chapter in their lives, so that they can move on.

Sure, sure, sure . . . come the murmurings . . . closure, yes . . . moving on, yes, that's it . . . moving on . . . (they repeat without thinking). You have to move on . . .

Therapy as placebo: a medicine given to humour or gratify a patient, rather than exercise any curative effect. An inactive substance administered in a double-blind trial. *Placebo*: I will please. What about the *ethics* of pleasing, of double-blinding, of humouring and gratification? Nothing. A contradiction in terms.

In response to the question of ethics, we can formulate three incompatible ethical levels. (1) The level of the autonomous subject, the Aristotelian or Kantian level of the 'Ought', which informs codes of ethics for psychological practitioners, for instance. (2) At the level of desire itself, the Lacanian ethics of the extreme. My not giving ground to *my desire* in an otherwise glacial universe of the impersonal Other — the narcissistic imperative becomes the necrophilic imperative.

Finally, there is a *third* level, the level of an *a priori* openness to the Other, a radical *ex*-posure (like Coupland's survivors above) which *faces* the impossible, the world as evil.

For Levinas, the power of ethics is entirely Other to the power of identity fashioned by therapy culture. It escapes and explodes these synthesising, centralising forces. This third level of ethics tears through all essences and totalities. Ethics is anarchic, subverting any provisional codes, staring at us accusingly through the naked face of the other against whom there is no defence and no escape. It shatters any sense of ethical complacency. Ethics is the *first* philosophy. It is *this* ethical sense that is entirely foreign to therapy.

What is ethical is violent. This accusation which leaves me devastated by its violating effraction requires the intervention of the third that comes between *that* face and me. The third is the Law which mediates what is *im*-mediate and shattering. It forbids the violence bound up with the over and excessive presence of Being. However, the Law creates a cover which the ethical will repeatedly blow open in its infinite negativity. The Law is a secondary process, distilled from the infinite proximity of the primary relation, and by its birth perjures (*parjure*)[14] itself. Calculations, comparisons, codes cut across the absolutely unique encounter of the face to face. The other is marginalised, ceases to exist. For ten people to die on British roads every day becomes 'acceptable', a necessary price to pay for the generalised law in favour of the freedom of movement.

If the Law by its inception blinds itself to unicity, how much more complicitous is therapy culture itself in its banal strategies and its pretensions to get to the heart of things? Therapy is no more than a reprocessing plant where the spent fuel of lives is recycled for further use in the war of the social. Perhaps you will be able to share your feeling with us? Silence!

How can psychoanalysis retain some trace of this effraction, this infinite response-ability for the other, or this absolute proximity of Being? Not by being more caring, empathetic or sympathetic. *Not* by making any assumptions about what the other needs. There is no new skill we must develop or position we must adopt. This ethics is never something we can be. Psychoanalysis is helpless in front of this ethical demand.

Levinas' ethics parallels the *primary* repression of the erotic for psychoanalysis that founds the subject, desire and the Law. Just as the foreclosed erotic will haunt the subject, so, therefore, will the ethical. Freud's myth of the murder of the Father of prehistory is an ever-present crime. This primordial trauma that grounds history and the Law, creating an illusion of peace and stability, comes at a cost of a permanent sense of accusation and discontent. Just as the law is the inverse of desire, so it is also the inverse of the ethical.

The account of Abraham's willingness to sacrifice Isaac illustrates at the most extreme point this paradox of the ethical. Abraham is willing to sacrifice Isaac in absolute obedience to God, but in a secret betrayal of all reason, law and morality. A father is ready to put to death his loving son because the Other asks or orders him without any explanation. Abraham is faithful to God only via his absolute treachery to his family and to all human values. As Derrida says 'I offer a gift of death' every time duty or responsibility bind me specifically to an other in his or her singularity. Consequently, I am bound to betray others, an infinite number of them.' As soon as I enter into a relation with the other, with the gaze, look, request, love, command, or call of the other, I know I can respond only by sacrificing ethics, that is, by sacrificing whatever obliges me to also respond, in the same way, in the same instant, to all the others' (Derrida, 1992, p. 68). Furthermore, I can never *justify* or excuse my sacrifice: why I respond here and not there, to this other and not that other. I have nothing to say about it. Nothing can be said about it.

At the last moment, when Abraham has said to God, 'Here I am,' and with the knife poised over Isaac, God reprieves Abraham: 'Lay not thine hand upon the lad . . . for now I know that thou fearest God' (Genesis 22.12). Abraham is both absolutely responsible and irresponsible at the same time. As Derrida comments, '[He] speaks to us of the paradoxical truth of our responsibility and of our relation to *the gift of death* of each instant' (p. 79).

Psychoanalysts can never be complacent about their work. The analyst is caught on every boundary: of responsibility and irresponsibility; of being in the Clearing on the Way *and* in the Night; of being fulfilled, yet being haunted by the ethical; of speaking and breaking the background silence; of openly hiding in secret.

Decadence

Any alternative, that disavows the haunting, that is content merely with *speaking* and consoling, can be described as decadent, allowing a falling down, decaying, unravelling. Decadence is easy and entropic, as effortless as free-fall. Take the example of the Esalen Institute for Human Potential. What they regarded as a 'successful' experiment during the 1970s was run with the nuns of the Convent of the Immaculate Heart in Los Angeles. Here, techniques of sexual liberation resulted in three hundred nuns asking to be released from their vows. The small remainder becoming radical lesbian nuns. This merely foreshadows the current autolysis of the Church (in America and Ireland) due, not to therapeutic attack from the outside, but to paedophilia and collapse from within.

Truth and Reconciliation.

> Can you tell us in your own words what happened . . . in those terrible incidents . . . take your time? . . . [silence].
>
> He will speak eventually . . . it's a matter of time . . . he will speak.

Why speak? Why talk? For whose benefit? The 'talking cure'? Talking betrays, in the double sense of *tradere*, to deliver up, to reveal a secret, but also to disclose in breach of trust, to expose what should remain hidden. Talking dissimilates. To attempt the impossible, namely, to say what actually happened, betrays, contradicts the ineluctable Real of the event. To say, to speak, leaves the Night behind to enter the light of therapeutic discourse with all its goodwill, complacency and knowing — its peace-keeping role, peace enforcing.

Truth *and* Reconciliation, without even the decency or courtesy of a gap between the two terms. One follows the other, without even a thought for what the (explosive) truth might do, what *saying it* might open up: a depth of grief where forgetting would be inhuman, yet remembering is constant torture.

The Czech philosopher, Jan Patocka, defines decadence as life losing its grasp, 'on the innermost nerve of its functioning process, [being] disrupted at its innermost core so that, while thinking itself full, it is actually draining and laming itself with every step and act' (Patocka, 1990, p. 97). A society, he suggests is decadent if it functions to encourage a decadent life, that is a life addicted to what is inhuman by its very nature.

And Patocka was a victim of this same inhumanity when he was tortured and murdered by the Stasi. Is psychoanalysis itself decadent as it encourages just this loosening of the grasp, a paradoxical 'liberation', the subversion of the Master discourse, the movement from symbolic consistency to its excremental remainder?

Psychoanalysis: *not giving ground to one's desire*, the loosening of bonds, the deferral of meaning, there is no Other of the Other therefore, *no* guarantee, *no* innermost core or nerve to lose anymore. Psychoanalysis *is* disruption of innermost functioning, just as language itself disrupts and defers. Psychoanalysis in the university, institute or academy is a long way from suffering which curls up with itself alone in the dark in silence.

Psychoanalysis has become indifferent in its coldness (or its softness) and the radical ethical position (level three) an irrelevance along the road to the fetishisation of desire, of *das Es*, the inhuman.[15] Beyond psychoanalysis, beyond the unconscious, desire and freedom and the transvaluation of values, there already looms perfection, the ultimate metadiscourse, the base sequence of the genetic code, and a new *base* molecular ethics. All ethical codes will be replaced by the genetic code. The psychoanalytic insistence on the subject and its recent and paradoxical self-immolation (the death of the subject), has ironically prepared the way for *psycho*-therapy to be swept away by *geno*-therapy. No more, the metaphorical translation of the unconscious, but instead, the *metonymical transcription* of the genome; no longer the guilt of having given ground relative to one's desire, but the bio-ethical imperative: to act in conformity with your genes. The ineluctable and the smart move, will be away from the approximation and inefficiency of 'psychic cleansing' and 'emotional intelligence' (via therapy) towards the pure eugenic and final form: 'genetic cleansing' and 'artificial intelligence'.

Notes

1. A much shorter version of this chapter was presented as a paper at a clinical meeting of the Irish Forum for Psychoanalytic Psychotherapy (I.F.P.P.) in December 1993. It subsequently was published in the *I.F.P.P. Journal, Vol. 4*, No. 1, pp. 33-48.

6. Al Qaeda is our current form of the Other.

3. *Das Ding*. Our desire, marked by the strictures of the signifier, is bound to drive beyond the pleasures of the phenomenal world, our world, the familiar world, towards the Thing which has been lost to the world forever. The Thing is that which can never be recovered for the order of meaning, it is therefore obscene, off the scene of human life. The tragic and the aesthetic are precisely this confrontation/encounter with the nothing to which desire brings us.

4. This is the classical view, expounded by O. Fenichel (1946, p. 376).

5. Channel 4, Slaves in Paradise, October 12th, 1999.

6. *New Statesman*, 19.11.93.

7. London: *The Times*. May 16th, 1994.

8. In this paper, Richardson takes as his starting point the ethical dilemmas posed by Kierkegaard's consideration of Agamemnon's sacrifice of his daughter, Iphegenia, and Abraham's offering up of Isaac as a sacrifice. He then moves to the Socratic notion of 'living honourably', and then following Lacan in his seminar, *The Ethics of Psychoanalysis*, he turns to Aristotle and Kant. For Aristotle it is *eudaimonia* — to be blessed with a guiding spirit towards the supreme good, accepting that this involves finitude, choice, reason and accountability. For Kant, in *The Critique of Pure Reason*, duty is the key, the 'categorical imperative' of conscience that is rigorous and unconditional in its demand for obedience to the universal law and reason. According to Richardson, the nub of Kantian ethics is: 'Act in such a way as to respect humanity, whether in your own person or in that of another, always as an end and never only as a means' (Richardson, 1998, p. 20). He goes on to ask if the ethics of psychoanalysis is anything more than a general ethics applied to the psychoanalytic situation. For psychologists the emphasis is on responsibility for professional expertise towards the community but especially the dignity, rights, autonomy, confidentiality of the client. The American Psychoanalytic Association has a similar code of practice. Freud, himself does not refer to an ethics of psychoanalysis. Lacan alone claims that Freud's project was fundamentally an ethical one, namely, a radical ethics of (unconscious) desire: 'Have you acted in conformity with the desire that is in you?' (Lacan, 1959–60, p. 311). The ethical tradition has always considered the human subject as autonomous. No ethics, however, has taken on board the unconscious as Freud conceived it, or, the subject as barred (by the signifier) as Lacan elaborated. Evans summarises the Lacanian ethical position, which he says, 'separates psychoanalysis from suggestion; psychoanalysis is based on a basic respect for the patient's right to resist domination, whereas suggestion sees such resistance as an obstacle to be crushed' (Evans, 1996, p. 58).

9. In my experience, analysts with growing children begin to take a more conservative view of the neutrality of the therapist on this question of the analysand's desire, privately calling into question freedoms that not too long before they accepted without question.

10. For the Lacanians, affects are only an effect of language. Affects can only be grasped secondarily through language, insofar as they can be spoken. Life in its proximity and *im*-mediacy is missed and slips away into the Real of incomprehension and irrelevance.

11. I am not advocating less academic rigour or dilution of the discipline into simplistic formulae of 'conflict resolution' or any other appeals to populist psychologies and illusory notions of 'healing', moralist demands, in short to closure. Nor is there any requirement to popularise psychoanalysis. Only to limit its self-marginalisaton.

12. In this connection it is interesting that the people assigned to package the information for public consumption are called spin-*doctors*.

13. December 21st, 2001. An elderly nun in Dundalk was brutally attacked, raped then murdered by a nineteen-year-old boy (apparently with no motive), as she waited for a bus to take her to Cork to visit relatives for Christmas.

14. The English word, perjury, carries with it an almost willful intent to lie or mislead, whereas the French, *parjure*, implies the breaking of any oath, obligation, faith or trust whether intentional or not. In this sense the Law deceives not accidentally or intentionally, but intrinsically.

15. Putting these points to a Lacanian colleague was met with a shrug of the shoulders.

Chapter 3

The Feral Child, the Broken Family & the Virtual World

We must begin to love in order that we may not fall ill, and must fall ill if, in consequence of frustration, we cannot love. — Freud (1914), p. 69

Ours is rather like the situation of a man who has lost his shadow: either he has become transparent, and the light passes right through him or alternatively, he is lit from all angles, and overexposed and defenceless against all sources of light. We are similarly exposed on all sides to the glare of technology, images and information, without any way of refracting their rays . . .
— Baudrillard (1990), p. 44

Atomic Rights

A hundred years ago families were broken by the untimely death of a parent or a child, for whom there was no treatment available. Today families are more likely to be broken by freedom, a new kind of death by excess, for which no treatment is available. Parents cannot predict that their children will marry and settle down. Older parents cannot expect to become grandparents. One in five women do not have children. Families must anticipate radical separation, mobility and individualisation on a scale never witnessed before. On the smaller scale, everything within the family has become diffuse and indistinct: leisure or track suits double as pyjamas; trainers are worn by people who may never train; fat people overeat and pathologically thin people live in terror of food. Meanwhile food abounds. Mealtimes are all times and everyone now grazes from the fridge. Relationships are marked by a diffuse rage as conflicting freedoms collide. Homes and apartments have become filled with a bewildering array of sophisticated electronic circuitry and info-technology, most of it unused, with the older people afraid to approach it, old and young alike tricked into thinking it is about education for the new century. All this against a background of continuous noise: from the sports, leisure, sex and entertainment *global* market.

According to British Home Office statistics, the 43% of crime committed by young people is costing the nation £5bn. One in four boys will commit a crime; one in eight girls. Guy and Hope (aptly named!) in Martin Amis's *London Fields* have produced an infant monster in the shape of little Marmaduke: 'The moment came and Marmaduke sprang for the knife. After a fierce struggle beneath the table Guy disarmed him and climbed to his feet, holding his nose where Marmaduke had bitten it' (Amis, 1989, p. 83). Indeed the child is the result of a monstrous liberal hypocrisy and complacency, sent up by Amis, whereby the very wealthy Guy and Hope can each give £15,000 to *Save the Children*, and then complain 'What about our child? Who's going to save him?' (p. 85). No one can, it seems! He is in a state of permanent tantrum silenced only by a parental one. 'For years they had worried about the kind of world they were bringing their child into. Now they worried about the kind of child they were bringing into their world' (p. 88).

We have come a long way from this news-clip of the 1950s from the BBC:

> At half-past eight there wasn't a cloud in the sky as Bill went off to work and Betty settled William the baby in his pram in the front garden to get the early morning sun. I hope he sleeps this morning and gives me a chance to get on with the work, she was thinking. Of course, while she was getting Elizabeth ready and packing her off to school, she was mentally reviewing all she had to do, but then this was no more than she had to do every Monday morning and she wasn't depressed . . . And so on.

We could not be further from Frank McCourt's, *Angela's Ashes, A memoir of a Childhood*:

> The master, Mr. Benson, is very old. He roars and spits all over us every day. He tells us we have to know the catechism backwards, forwards and sideways. He tells us we're hopeless, the worst class he has ever had for First Communion but as sure as God made little apples he'll make Catholics of us, he'll beat the idler out of us and the Sanctifying Grace into us.
>
> Brendan Quigley, known as Question Quigley, raises his hand . . . Sir, he says, what's Sanctifying Grace?
>
> The master rolls his eyes to heaven. He's going to kill Quigley. Instead he barks at him. Never mind what's Sanctifying Grace, Quigley. That's none of your business. You're here to learn the Catechism and do what you're told. You're not here to be asking questions. There are too many people wandering the world asking

questions and that's what has us in the state we're in, and if I find any
boy in the class asking questions I won't be responsible for what happens. Do you hear me Quigley? (McCourt, 1997, pp. 129-30).

The remorseless interrogation of culture, since Quigley and
Benson's time has gone on apace until *all* the answers are available.
Now, nothing is hidden. Schoolmaster Benson already had more
than a hunch that the game, the game of repression was over, and
that he would not be responsible for what was about to happen — the orgy
of tearing down. Question Quigley has heard, but takes no notice.
He has no need to. The tide was hopelessly against Benson. If he was
still alive today, he might probably be paraded as a child abuser with
no one prepared to defend him, and many of Quigley's classmates
are claiming compensation from the traumatic memories that 'to this
day affect our lives, so much so that we can't get the things that
Benson did to us out of our minds. Our lives have been ruined.' Or he
might have gone the demented way of the exemplary school master
Raphael Bell, passionate believer in Irish tradition, yet unable to
accept change, unable to tolerate the things in which be believed,
being mocked by a younger generation. He ends up in *The Dead
School* (Pat McCabe) teaching imaginary pupils.

Ironically, the tide is against even Guy and Hope. Even their sur-
real, postmodern, ecological relationship is torn through by untram-
melled rage. And our post-World War II mother, happy to be at
home, presents only a manic facade of delightful sunny happiness as
a defence against the depressive isolation of modern featureless
housing estates where the nuclear family abstracted from the larger
community and diverted for a time by consumer durables was about
to implode in a haze of mass medical tranquillisation. Those mothers
became depressed before their daughters took to the streets and
demanded liberation.

Those of us who have lived through this period of transition may
well ask in disbelief: what has happened? Where has authority
gone? How could it have gone? How could it have gone so quickly?
On the left, authority is derided as synonymous with the old repression. A few shreds may still be left to strip away. The left believes in
the free market of lifestyles. The right feels that the State must be dis-
mantled, with its pretension to public service and public education,
which stands in the way of the free operation of the Market. The
plain fact is that people feel less and less inclined to agree, to accept
or wield authority in any area of life. The whole notion of authority
has quite simply been dropped. It has fallen away. Or it has undergone an *involution* and its power has returned in its subatomic form
— namely the empowerment of each atom — atomic rights. Ours is
the era of atomic rights. Authority has been replaced by a market-

place of rights in which each group, or individual, or child, or animal, or indeed perhaps atoms must insist on their rights and their
personal freedom. From this hypermoral perspective, we can all
claim that we are victims. You must have been victimised: make
your claim.

At a recent conference on psychotherapy and the public sphere,
concern was expressed by many participants about the whole question of authority in relation to *children*. There was a lingering doubt
as to the safety of children in a world of atomic rights, although, at
the same time you could detect a feeling of queasiness about whispering this to one another: were we not showing a lack of faith in the
humanist project? Was it just age — we were all around fifty — the
age at which privately at least lack of faith in atomic rights can begin
its steep upward trajectory, especially if *that* generation prided itself
on the illusion of creating this 'revolution' itself.

A careful argument against this fear of freedom and complexity
has been presented by Barry Richards, taking an optimistic view of
modern popular culture. From his psychodynamic point of view,
some cultural forms such as sport offer a chance for children and others to enjoy drive or impulse excitement bounded by containment,
the rules of the game. Acknowledging, that the old hierarchical
forms of authority are on the wane, new cultural forms — the
televisual culture, the therapeutic culture — are new sources of values, *no longer imposed by any ideological elite*. Soaps dramatise moral
issues and the emotional life of ordinary relationships. Psychotherapy and counselling have created a therapeutic culture that privileges feeling, subjectivity and identity. Richards also notes that
ethical issues increasingly affect the world of advertising, commerce
and charity, particularly in relation to the environment. He even
envisages the emergence of 'moral communities of consumption'
(Richards, 1994) whereby we might boycott companies that exploit
third world labour. Richards considers that the televisual and the
therapeutic cultures come together in the focus on (political) *person-
alities*. We want to scrutinise our leaders for their *emotional* qualities:
can they be trusted; how do they act under stress; how do they treat
others; etc.? He claims the public is able to see beyond the promotional videos of our leaders.

However, this analysis is inadequate. From a more radical *psychoanalytic* standpoint there is no commensal relationship between culture and the individual. Psychoanalysis is correctly implicated in
sponsoring the development of the therapeutic culture of subjectivity. Freud was clearly the modern *initiator* of this development,
although he should not be held responsible for its excesses in the
present. Freud was also the theoriser, arguably the best and only

theoriser of human subjectivity. Even a recent *Scientific American* article, critical of the 'talk-therapies', acknowledges Freud's genius as a theoretician.

Freud always maintained that Oedipus was the pivot around which his whole theory of neurosis turned. Implicit in Freud is the notion that the human subject is always *larger* than life. His theory of the drives, the sexual and aggressive drives, implies a continuous force impelling the human subject beyond what might contain it within cultural norms. Against any progressive notion of an accommodation of the subject within given cultural constraints, Freud posits an essential *beyond* of human desire. Human desire can never be adequately represented *within* culture, it drives beyond constraint towards anarchy and asociality.

The Crucible

To be sure, in the crucible of the family, the drives are laboriously tamed, educated, transformed, into a *human* form, in short, repressed and divided within themselves. The metaphor of the crucible is central here. The crucible is a pot or furnace, fired with coal, coke, oil or gas, in which ores are melted to produce pure metals. Historically, the family in some form has been the arena in which this complex metamorphosis occurs.

Cultural conditions have changed so radically, it is hard to believe now that Winnicott said: 'I assume all the time a mother person holding the situation, day by day, week in, week out' (Winnicott, 1988, p. 78). The outcome, Winnicott tells us, is a transitional space — 'a neutral area of experience which will not be challenged' (Winnicott, 1958, p. 239). Then comes a necessary *dis*-illusionment beginning at weaning, and developing through inevitable losses, the reality principle, in Freudian terms, the introduction of a cut (symbolic castration) initiated by the father, which gives depth and what Lacan has called 'affective density'. But to a degree this inaugural experience of primary illusionment stays with us as a partial *shield* against pain and loss. But the *two* movements are essential. On the one hand to be in this private privileged erotic relationship with the mother (figure) which grounds the infant in its own *special* desirability and provides this illusion of security, and, on the other hand, the break-up of this, the failure, the unavoidably tragic loss of unity initiated by the father (figure) who will insert the child into the cultural order under the law. The child moves from having a supreme place to taking up a *limited* place within the social fabric. Destabilisation of this formative Oedipal[1] process leads to emotional extremism, and to the beginning of the end of the illusion, which made life bearable, even enjoyable. Many commentators have pointed out that this transitional space has collapsed into a frenzy of vapid gratifications characteristic of the narcissistic personality, whose flatness, hyperactivity and emotional coldness are all there to seduce us away in simulations of self. Everything is then forced and confused into a near likeness of itself.

In the crucible, the father intrudes to separate the mother and child, and to introduce the child against his will, his desire, into the Law of culture. A 'fight' ensues in which the child will suffer itself to take on (identify with) the mores of the culture represented by the father. The child will be inserted into human culture. From then on the child will be forever divided within itself. On the one side will be the unconscious with its repressed contents and drives, and on the other will be the father, now internalised as the superego. This is the initiating point that will enable the child to take on further identifications with others in school and the wider community. The matter is never settled, and fathers and sons, mothers and daughters will always be divided within themselves and against each other, suffering, loving and hating, in measures that always threaten to be larger than life.

Against Richards, what is envisaged here is an intensely dramatic process requiring *real* people. Psychoanalysis emphasises that the child identifies with the *body and mind* of his parents in a milieu of constant encounter and mutual antagonism. The question for us is: can our re-ordered families, broken and reconstructed, or just broken, at the same time both intense and dispersed, provide this crucible for the Oedipal meltdown that yields the ore of a civilised human being? There are in fact two stages of meltdown. The first is during early childhood, the Oedipal phase proper, and the second during adolescence which acts, Freud suggests, as a 'deferred-action', a *Nachtraglichkeit*, that is a real working-over of what earlier was unassimilable and now can be better understood. Have the significant others in the child's life become too thin on the ground to provide these identifications in early childhood and later during adolescence? If the answer to this question is yes, as many now believe, how can the more psychically distant and diluted form of the so-called 'role-model', or *image* of the other (the sports hero, the rock star, the soap character, the 'personality') possibly stand in a *real bodily* way for the missing or transient parent? How can these simulated forms create a real encounter that goes to the heart of things? How can an adolescent engage with a poster or a screen in lieu of a real other to fight with and destroy?

If the struggle of social relations, of contact, mutuality, engagement and conflict has seeped away, then we must add a post-

Freudian theory coming from Melanie Klein to envisage a further development. When children deferred to adults, the very harsh superego of early childhood that Klein discovered in developing her 'play-technique', underwent some modification during adolescence. At this time the superego could be continually tested against the strength of real authority figures in the shape of other relatives, grandparents, teachers, priests, youth club leaders, police and so on, that children looked up to. Contact and conflict with these figures offered at least the possibility of mitigation of these strong irrational unconscious guilt feelings stemming from the drive phantasies associated with early childhood.

The imbalance created by the great shift in values from self-restraint to self-indulgence has lead, I have argued (Weatherill, 1994) to the uncovering of the *infantile prototype* of the superego, namely the archaic superego. This cannot be understood as an agency having anything to do with morality. It opposes the drives, but indeed in a very *driven* way, according to the brutal principle of the talion. Freud had already drawn attention to the severity of the superego, indeed its 'sadism' and 'merciless violence', in the cases of the obsessional and the melancholic. Klein further deepened our understanding of the primitive superego, 'immeasurably harsher and more cruel than that of the older child or the adult. . . . We get to look upon the child's fear of being devoured, or cut up, or torn to pieces, or its terror of being surrounded and pursued by menacing figures' (Klein, 1933, pp. 248–9). These terrors arise *not* from the severity of the *actual* parents, but from the rageful aggression of the infantile drives now misconstrued as attacking him from the *outside*, against which they were originally projected. These cause the young child to suffer persecutory anxiety — the anxiety of being cut through, or cut to pieces. When rage is at its height, children never tire of 'tearing and cutting up, breaking and wetting and burning all sorts of things like paper, matches, boxes, small toys, all of which represent (unconsciously) parents, brothers, sisters and bodies and breasts, and this rage for destruction alternates with attacks of anxiety and guilt' (p. 255). Now if parents and significant adults remain available and reliable, the child can continue to play his aggressive symbolic games and work though these primitive anxieties without ever becoming aware or troubled by them to any significant extent.

With the lessening of the repressive cohesiveness of the old superego deriving from the Oedipus Complex, and the stripping away of all the old authority that has been fought for so strongly and so consistently by an earlier generation, there comes an unexpected reversal. What was dreamt of as liberation did not bank on the irrational *vengeance* of the archaic superego. An increasing number of children have no opportunity to test their terrors against the reality of a relatively benign, strong and contained environment. Instead they become enslaved to drives and counterdrives, hyperstimulated and depressed.

Uncontained, they act-out. To an extreme degree, they will try to *force* a reaction from such weakened authorities as remain, in homes and schools. They will be incredibly attention-seeking, hyperactive, difficult, uncontrollable, repeatedly inviting retaliation. According to Klein:

> Children who were unconsciously expecting to be cut to pieces, beheaded, devoured and so on, would feel compelled to be naughty and get punished, because the real punishment, however severe, was reassuring in comparison with the murderous attacks which they were continuously expecting from phantastically cruel parents (Klein, 1934, p. 258).

Children *want* punishment so that they can compare phantasy with reality. Without this reality check they are bound to push phantasy until they find a limit — the police and judicial system.

Freedom from the old repressive taboos has meant *increased* levels of anxiety. All change brings anxiety, but this 'liberation' from all restraint has involved increasing numbers of children in an *excess* of anxiety. And we might link this sort of psychoanalytic theorising with the well known facts about children's suffering — increased eating disorders, juvenile crime, psychiatric admissions and at younger ages, earlier and increased drug abuse and underachievement at school. Child care professionals will readily admit that levels of child distress are far greater than they were only a decade ago, more depressions, more behaviour problems and so on.

To the psychoanalytic mind, contemporary theorising and policy making in relation to children and the family continually misses that element in human subjectivity that is *irrepressible*, namely that dimension of the drive. The widespread belief is that education, skills training for parenting, lessons in 'emotional intelligence', teaching children about their rights, democratic families, and all manner of educational domestication, will bring progress and individual freedom. All these rational solutions, coming from the final phases of the enlightenment tradition in the West, fail to take account of the *unchanging real* of human relationships. These have always been based on power, force and hierarchy, and yet in the special case of children we have pretended to relinquish these.

The ideal of child autonomy has nothing to do with childhood and nothing to do with autonomy. It has much to do with parental autonomy *from* children — parental rights to freedom and enjoyment, rights to be free *of* children who can look after themselves. In reality, it is the end of childhood. Without the necessary repression belonging to Oedipus (and the strong family structure), the child is enslaved by the over-close proximity of its passions, with no space from which to think, create and live in freedom.

During medieval times, the child was either not represented, or represented as a little adult. It was only during the modern period that the notion of 'child' or 'childhood' came slowly to be recognised. And only in the middle part of the last century was the category 'adolescent' or 'teenager' invented. In the new century, these terms are changing again, and childhood may be ending altogether. At the same time, with a massive guilty conscience, we privilege childhood in the extreme.

Three Orders of Childhood

Put simply we can delineate three orders of childhood.

1) The pre-modern or traditional: here children were owned as economic objects. They had no rights. To have large numbers of children brought economic benefits to the family. Large numbers were important for another reason — so many of them died. In colonial America for instance more than half did not reach the age of ten.

2) The modern: here children were idealised, cherished, domesticated, disciplined, brought centre stage, with their rights enshrined in law. Wanted, planned for, showered with love, there were many fewer of them, and now instead of bringing economic benefit to the family, they became increasingly an economic burden.

3) The postmodern: children as autonomous, freed from what was deemed parental control or abuse, children exist on their own, allegedly 'making their own choices', but *with nothing to separate them from the market*. 'Happy', with agencies of the State and the Market that have overthrown Oedipus, they chant in our faces: *Don't patronise us — children are people too.*

In the first phase children made money for the family. In the second they had money, pocket money. In the third, they make money for themselves. In the first phase they were under parental domination. In the second, brutal control gave way to educational and moral control and solicitude (the old paternal superego). In the final phase, peer control and market forces vie for *total* control (the archaic superego). This third phase is the end of childhood, the *feral* phase. In Ireland and other countries, all three levels can coexist at this transitional time. Phase one is still a feature of demoralised rural communities.[2] Phase two would be clung to by middle-class families, who feel themselves in danger of being overtaken by phase three, a classless phenomenon of anonymous urban and suburban cultures world-wide, where the adults, instead of watching out for and watching over children, feel threatened and powerless in the face of other children and their own, who are out of control.

Phase three is coincident with the child returned to the status of object. When it comes to children's culture and commodities aimed only at children, most concede that socialisation of children is really increasingly about a cynical expansion of corporate global interests — the exploitation of children as consumers. No debt, no castration, no subjectivity, but instant gratification — the (human) right to demand what they want and to be happy — now! The children's market in the US is reliably calculated at $200bn. There has been an immense corporate research effort to find out precisely what children want, to speak to them in their own language, to design toys and products that will exactly stimulate and gratify their desires. What is essential is 'product tie-in'. In the 1990s every new product was launched through TV — not through the ads, but the programmes themselves. In the 1980s in the US (not UK), there was Reaganite deregulation of children's TV. Toy manufacturers were free to create and market identities and personalities for children to engage in fantasy with. They amplified the gender split: Action Man and the violent resolution of conflict; Cindy and Barbie, dolls who want to be attractive and be the centre of attention.

All this industry to fill an unbounded space opened up by spiralling demand free of any restraints. Michael Rosen, the author of *The Penguin Book of Childhood*, suggests that there have been ads specifically aimed at children throughout the 20th Century, Dinkies, Meccano, etc. For Rosen, it is just a question of degree and volume. Neil Postman's book, *The Disappearance of Childhood*, was reprinted after 10 years. He points-out that children were traditionally kept from the secrets of the adult world — intimate sexual and medical knowledge. This we understand psychoanalytically, as the repression central to Oedipus. However, TV, video, the Net, DVD all make pornography freely available. Therefore, there is no point anymore in eavesdropping on adult conversation. Why should we insult them by treating them like children?

Even children's books, once thought to be safe and situated firmly in transitional space, now have to deal with the gritty realities of homelessness, domestic violence, etc. At one time, children's literature explored the great themes, which took children out of their time and their immediate circumstances. Now, it is widely argued, children should not be protected from what they see on a London street.

Look at Hansel and Gretel: a story of two parents who want to kill their children, and another parent figure who wants to eat them up! This line of argument completely misses the point about the symbolic nature of so-called brutal fairy tales (see Bettleheim). But to push the point further, why not video games, with their very reduced narrative, the emotional hit, always unsatisfying, so you keep playing? And why not, moving towards the zero of narrative, channel zapping, channel surfing, from so-called 3 minute culture to a few second culture? This increasing fragmentation, acceleration and immediacy are essential to disperse the excessive affects unleashed by the end of Oedipus. The time is one of total restlessness, irritability and rage on the edge of futility.

Our view of childhood has shifted decisively within the modern period, from believing children to be bearers of Original Sin to being blessed with innocence and in need of protection. This shift is reflected in a complex way within psychoanalytic theorising. The recognition of the perverse infantile sexuality that must come under the law of the father during Oedipus, versus the emphasis on holding, reverie and mothering and the creating of the transitional space that we have noted above.[3] Modern children were to be cherished. This shift began with the middle class and then spread to the working classes — children working, being exploited in cotton factories, in chimneys, in mines, were all seen as being at odds with nature. Intense campaigning for reform in the late 19th and early 20th Centuries, resulted in children being excluded from adult working environments, from public houses, etc. They were felt to be too exposed to the adult pornographic world. Enclosures were made for them — safe havens, playgrounds, schools, special zones. The decisive shift was from level one to the privileged domain of level two.

But this couldn't last. This privacy is no longer 'a neutral area that will not be challenged'. Ironically, this segregation, setting children apart, has made them easier to exploit commercially and to study scientifically. Once everything is known about childhood, that is the end of childhood. Children have never been more exposed to the glare of everything. Children like adults are made to speak and know about everything. This violates Winnicott's notion of the subject's privacy and 'urgent need *not to be found*' (Winnicott, 1963, p. 187; added emphasis) and of 'the primordial experience occurring in solitude' (p. 190).

We have come the full circle. Winnicott and others were to privilege the inaugural moment of primary illusionment at just the time when its provision was about to disappear, not via the prophylactic way of Oedipus which makes loss almost bearable, but via a violent excess which turns loss into rage. This real slipping away of the nuclear self that we have described is marked by every last ditch stand for individuality — *my* freedoms, *my* rights, *my* pleasure, *my* sexuality — as a consolation for the end of all of these. If we take Grotstein's (1978) model of mental space, we have moved from the three dimensions of the Oedipal structuring to a two dimensional loss of density (narcissistic), and may be approaching the linear or the single point of maximal intensity, the zero of mental life. As Baudrillard says, we are approaching the era of 'total self-seduction', the era of 'a digital Narcissus instead of a triangular Oedipus' (Baudrillard, 1979, p. 175).

Children are hit from *three* sides. Firstly, they can no longer expect their drives to be contained, encountered and controlled by either parents or teachers, who were part of a real that no longer exists. Secondly, world-wide, under the auspices of the UN Convention on the Rights of the Child, the global ideological shift has been towards the autonomy of the child. The therapeutically inspired liberation movement now extends to children, embodied for instance in the ironically called 'stay safe' programme — that is, staying safe *from* parents and adults of all kinds. And, thirdly, they are caught in the virulent glare of a continuous global hypersexuality and violence. All that is left is a massive *performance* of childhood which envisages children being able to *choose* their drugs, their safe sex, their information, their skills. The best children will, as always, dutifully do what is expected of them, only now it's much harder, and an increasingly significant minority (20% in some urban areas) are removing themselves and becoming feral, becoming waste from the system. All that is on offer to them is their rights — not their rights to a real world with its human drama of encounter and loss, but to a synthetic electronic world of the market and its inexorable play and entertainment against the abyss. Since the Bulger case, it has been widely alleged that children will act out the violence they see on the screen. This may be so, but what is more likely is that their violence is directed at the screen itself and its transmission of an indifferent culture. In a programme about the recent spate of high-school killings in the States, one young adult male is seen on his own out in the country-side shooting with his automatic weapon at a television set positioned on a hillside, some distance away. As he hits the shattered set repeatedly, he tells us with chilling accuracy that he is 'killing the baby-sitter of the American family'.

According to psychoanalytic theory, the Oedipus complex creates *two* major differentiations. Firstly, it establishes the difference between the generations; secondly, the difference between the sexes. Consequently, the term 'child' means nothing except in differentiation to the term 'parent'. Similarly, the term 'man' only has meaning in relation to the term 'woman'. These differences are created by the Oedipus complex. For instance, a father is radically different to a son; a mother is different from a daughter. Each has to assume a position vis-à-vis the other of the different generation. The son, for instance, has to acknowledge the father as father. With the end of Oedipus, and the new pretense of equality, all the differences collapse into each other. The term 'child' becomes increasingly meaningless — he or she becomes just another autonomous atom.

Essentially, the Oedipus complex enshrines, at its heart, the law against incest. It is synonymous with the incest taboo. Contemplating its removal may implicitly legitimise sexual and abusive relations between the generations. If there is no difference *between* the generations, why should a father and daughter, for instance, not have sex together? Add to this: if both have been starved of love in an atomistic society, will they not be naturally drawn to each other in desperation? Similarly, fathers and sons, also so-called care workers and those casualties of atomism, children 'in care', why should they not abuse each other? All kinds of unravellings become possible. Our present revulsion at these kinds of perversions, underlies in this respect at least our implicit recognition that an Oedipal line must indeed continue to be drawn, so that the daughter must continue to be protected in her status as 'daughter' and as 'child'. Without this line a plague indeed descends.

Continuous Revolutions

There are a number of assertions that can be made:

(1) There is now no recoverable form of *traditional* family life. The erosion of the extended family and social fabric in general has occurred over a long period, but most recently in two cultural revolutions. The first during the 1960s when the family was regarded on the New Left as an 'ideological conditioning device' (Cooper, 1971) to be subverted and dispersed into a multiplicity of lifestyle forms. The second, during the 1980s in which the New Right emerged advocating radical economic freedoms — 'there is no such thing as society' . . . 'greed is good'. The fall of the Wall in 1989 ushered in global capitalism. These revolutions followed on the devastating effects of two world wars.

Some post-war British psychoanalytic theorists became intensely aware and concerned about the stability and reliability of the early familial environment for infant care in a culture that was already unravelling. The breakdown[4] of the family (more broadly, the end of traditional cultures world-wide under the impact of the modernising process) leads to the loss of ongoing living contact and cohesiveness between parent and infant, and also a loss in the continuous education and integration of the emotional life, which has long term implications.[5] In a sense the ego itself is being lost for want of support in its formative years. We can no longer be sure of Bion's assertion that 'like the earth, he [the child] carries with him an atmosphere, albeit a mental one, which shields him from the mental counterpart of the cosmic and other rays at present supposed to be rendered innocuous to men, thanks to the physical atmosphere' (Bion, 1992, p. 192).

(2) Human solidarity, whether local, factory, class or familial, has disappeared. Since the end of the 1950s in the West, we have noticed the beginning of the end of working class movements, and the slow break-up of the body politic into competing groupings that ceased to define their interests in terms of a better society, but rather in competing terms of narrow self-interest and claims to victimisation. The British miners strike in 1984 was the last flicker of human solidarity. Now, each wants his individualised freedoms. Freedoms are the absolute good. Commitment has gone in favour of limited contractual relationships. The old restrictive bonds of the social have dissolved into a kind of Brownian motion or kinetic energy of communication, networking and interactivity. Therapy is the lubricant. It creates a semblance of human solidarity to hide the void at the heart of the social.

(3) The sexualisation of everything has become the motor of therapeutic culture, literally it material substance. What was heretofore implicit, repressed and hidden, is now explicit, in-your-face, casual, violently opened. Marcuse dubbed this desublimation. For Baudrillard, 'Everything is sexualised before disappearing' (Baudrillard, 1983, p. 55). By this reversal, that is the dedicated return to sexuality — we were supposed to leave it largely behind at the end of Oedipus, apart from the intermittent enjoyments of 'official' sexuality — everything imaginable must carry an erotic supplement, its own sexing up. It is no longer possible for adolescents to be 'awakened' by the awesome Otherness of Eros. Coarsened and banalised beyond measure, sex becomes more and more pure drive mechanics between depersonalised muscular orifices turbo-charged, as it were, for the job, a four-wheel-drive off-roader sexuality masquerading as freedom. Therapeutically recycled and cooled, sex is deemed 'recreational', even 'spiritual'.

Privacy, inner reserve involving the capacity to sublimate, is re-read by therapeutic culture as 'denial'. Equal access for all to everyone and everything means that privacy and reticence have become subversive, in need of therapeutic intervention. Probably, there are still surviving vestiges of secrecy in everyone, but we have learnt well (through work on ourselves) how to make the false self look true, to give all the appearences of transparency. Without boundaries, things can flow in and out without restriction, as has been dramatically represented by the incidence of rape and child sexual abuse. There are an estimated quarter of a million paedophiles in Britain facilitated by the latest global technologies for their gratification. These crimes tear into the primitive defences which stand guard over our secret invisibility. Ironically, sexuality still symbolises privacy, and it is around sexuality therefore that invasions — both psychical and physical — will occur, in a culture of total openness. With the liberation of sexuality in all forms come the liberation of perversion, of sexual *crimes*. The way of unlimited pleasuring has facilitated unlimited violation.[6] The negative potential here is unlimited in the new deregulated market, with sex slavery, trafficking, tourism, every unimaginable degradation is now possible.

Ours is a binary culture, where the switch of the sexual machine, which can run twenty-four-seven is either 'on' or 'off', 'open' or 'closed'. We're turned-on to more and more products and services, or, turned-off: at one moment, open — sexually voracious, predatory and exhausted. At another, bang closed — puritanical, inflexible and litigious.

(4) No more depth paradigms. Orthodox psychoanalysis, coming out of the modern tradition, always understood some notion of defence against the hidden or repressed unconscious formations. Interpretation and free association reveals something of the 'inner'. The movement was from surface to depth, from manifest to latent, from the false self to the true self, from ego to subjectivity, from persona to Self, and so on. But all depth models have disappeared. There is no origin to appeal to, no essence, no truth, no real as opposed to appearance, no authenticity to pit against inauthenticity and alienation, no signified under the signifier. In post-modernity, there are only surfaces, plays of light, reflections, refractions, diffractions, deferrals and language playing with itself. This is the end of psychoanalysis.[7] Or, worse, we are condemned to therapy interminably, both individually and culturally, with no appeal possible to deeper meanings, no bedrock of castration. Was this erasure of the referents a secret ploy of therapy culture to take over the planet. Wipe out any *point de capitons* and the world is yours. Remove all illusions and what then transpires is so horrendous that even therapy cannot cope, but it is all that we have left to help us.

The modern and postmodern exploration of nothingness of absolute zero, of nihilism, the *excavated* centre around which we now blindly stumble, cannot be refuted. Living ephemerality, instability, illegitimacy, and recycling of everything, with no ultimate point of reference, no authorisation, and no longer any appeal to Logos, we are caught in the glare of rigorous disillusionment against which there can be no trivial consolation and no appeal.

It could be argued that the relentless persuit of meanings, is in itself an intensely ethical project, which owes a debt to the traditions that, at the same time, it is annihilating. Should not this process call forth a more intense desire to find new meanings beyond meaning-lessness? Perhaps. However, any appeal to ultimacy on our part, or any other appeal to commonsense, to the obvious meanings in life, or the traditional interpretive consensus, and so on, cannot refute the (deconstructionist) argument. It cannot be refuted on its own terms. It can only be negated, mitigated, covered over by a variety of soft (therapeutic) strategies of *re*-covery.

(5) Chief amongst these is *feminisation*: in face of nihilism and the cultural fatalism of the West, there has been a counter-response — a cultural shift in favour of a maternal feminine — the velvet revolu-tion of connectedness, completeness and harmony.[8] In these glacial times, there is 'natural' drift or slide towards the maternal, towards a feminine ideal, the neutered form of the *a*-sexual. Gone are harsh dif-ferentiations and discriminations, in favour of the indiscriminate. Signs lose their difference and their meaning, like all terms within the soft embrace of the imaginary feminine principle of continuity and seamlessness — a magical world with no cut with no severance, the never never world of the ideal ego, of *indifference*. The wide-spread belief is that the feminine will heal everything, all the alleged damage of patriarchy. The horror of male violence, of all pain and hurt, will be dissipated by the aroma of therapy, whose healing vapours are everywhere, dissipating every anachronism. Only the feminine knows its own completeness and perfection. Leave the endless preoccupation with castration to the anxious male who has to be violent to be strong. The feminine is at the heart of therapy cul-ture and most of its practitioners are women. Dressed often in flow-ing garments, they talk confidently but very quietly of healing and weeping, of knowing and loving, of tenderness and understanding and your creativity — *let it flow*. All resistances will be overcome, what, after all is there to hide anymore? You can tell me, your true mother, your earth goddess mother. Even, the ground water of our culture has become feminised. Synthetic oestrogens abound in the over-enrichment of the environment. Phthalates cling-wrap our food, sealing in its highly-refined artificial goodness, causing even the sperm to turn on their heads, lose their virility, and give up in vast millions. You cannot swim against the tide.

(6) Sperm *without fathers*. Poverty, (male) unemployment, the marketisation of the workforce, families without fathers, communi-

ties without fathers, fathers without fathers, have all contributed to a generalised collapse, which, in psychoanalytic terms, is the loss of the space of this mythical Oedipal period, which, as we have emphasised, necessarily inscribes in us a *prophylactic* loss, guilt and a sense of indebtedness to the world. No one is indebted anymore. No one feels gratitude, only rancour. Marriage was there to bind men and women, however imperfectly, into the community. Through marriage the father was connected by law to the larger community, where he frequently became involved with teaching or instruction of the younger generation. Now, unbound, dislocated, rejected by Woman, there is an underclass of mainly working-class male youth, immature, unsocialised and withdrawn from any residual social structure. This is only the sharp visible end of a more generalised loss of the paternal function and any agreed notion of authority. Now, we are our *own* authorities.

However, family life has been chaotic and distressful since at least the mid-18th Century. In the early 19th Century there was concern about young men on the streets and what they might get up to, which was part of a general concern, then as now, about children in our large cities. Apprentices too, although they were looked after by a master, what happened to them when they went out on the street? Many will argue that our present concerns are not at all new.

. . . Or Worse

While Nietzsche had to live with 'the death of God', we, a stage further on in evolution, are to live more and more without God and without the father or without the 'paternal metaphor'. Lacan warned: *le père ou pire*. We are now in the domain of the worse. Experimenting on the edge without God, now, in apocalyptic mood, we venture forth without the father as well. Psychoanalysis came into being as the bourgeois ideal of the family was already in crisis at the end of the 19th Century.

Freud's case histories, no less, point to some deepening failure in the paternal function. With this little sample that Freud provided, we can see we were already in deep trouble. Dora's father was an impotent man, trying to have an affair with Herr K's wife. He contracted syphilis before he was married, was prone to illness all his life, when Dora was six he contracted TB, when she was ten he had a detached retina, and at twelve, he had his worst illness — a confusional attack, for which he sought help from Freud.

The Ratman's father was a good man, indeed a friend to his son, a military man, but a gambler with a gambling debt, a man who married for money not for love. Little Hans' father was more like a mother, full of patient understanding, but not able to symbolise castration in any way for his son. The Wolf-Man's father suffered from 'attacks of depression', not long after his parents were married. At six, he remembers going to see his father in the sanatorium, where the father would go from time to time for treatment for what Krapelin diagnosed as manic-depression. His father was a cultured intelligent man, but without humour. He died at 49 in Moscow, supposedly from an overdose of the tranquiliser Veronal (see Gardiner, 1971, p. 64), when the Wolf-Man was 21. In today's jargon, he was an absent father.

But if some fathers were collapsing, others were aware of this potential for exhaustion, and countered it with an excess in the other direction, only serving to underline the collapse already in process. Freud's analysis of Schreber's *Memoirs*, for instance, directed researchers to correlate Schreber's paranoia with his father's very influential writing on the necessity for extreme strictness in child rearing. Niederland (1984) returns to Schreber's father's writings, including editions of *Arztliche Zimmergymnastik* (Medical Indoor Gymnastics), as well as published and unpublished biographical material. The father's methods were not untypical of the time, the mid-19th Century. He was a doctor, lecturer, writer, educator and clinical instructor in the medical school of the University of Leipzig. He specialised in orthopaedics, and wrote about twenty books on the subject and guidelines for rearing children. He was a reformer, fanatically dedicated to his goals in the field of physical culture and health. He founded a cultist movement which lasts until the present time. According to Niederland, Dr Schreber's biographer, Ritter, expressing his admiration of both Dr Schreber and Hitler, saw in the former a sort of spiritual precursor of Nazism. Dr Schreber used his progressive methods on his own children, driving his two sons, not it seems his three daughters, into complete submission and passivity. One son, Gustav, committed suicide by shooting himself, and the other, as we know, became the celebrated paranoiac.

One way or another, there was no way out; fathers were marked men. Their time was up. Redundancy was in sight. Within psychoanalysis, as elsewhere, the ideological focus switched powerfully towards the mother. The British school was to emphasise the role of the mother — the pre-Oedipal mother — and was busy radically changing psychoanalysis, and therapy generally, into some version of a nurturing activity. As Phillips notes, 'Mothering has replaced dreaming as the royal road to the unconscious' (Phillips, 1993, p. 109). He is sceptical of this 'playing mothers' — 'the sphinx *without* a riddle' (p. 115; emphasis added).

Lacan alone spoke up for the father and the absolute value that should be placed on the 'tender virile identification'. However,

Lacan acknowledges: 'The resulting situation for this good father is a remarkably difficult one; *to a certain extent he is an insecure figure*' (Lacan, 1959–60, p. 181; emphasis added).

Speaking of neurosis as early as 1938, Lacan says that weak fathers problematise sublimation and creativity. With foresight, he warns, 'Impotence and the utopian spirit are the sinister godmothers who watch over the cradle of the neurotic and imprison his ambition' (Lacan, 1938, p. 46).

It was not actual fathers, but the *symbolic* father which was the crucial agency for Lacan. The *murdered* father of the primal horde, 'lives' on as this bearer of language, of differentiation, of meaning, of repression (the superego) on the one hand, and promise (the ego ideal) on the other. He is the 'spokesman', who explains the world. He is the one who acknowledges, legitimates, and underscores us. Without the agency of the father, things fall apart, the Imaginary register, as we have emphasised, becomes hyper-realised.

Borch-Jacobsen summarises the Lacanian position:

> ... the insolvency and 'narcissistic bastardising' of the father figure, the growing indistinguishability of the paternal function from the 'specular double', the 'tangential movement towards incest' in our societies. ... In short, it is the competitive, rivalrous world, revealed as the great traditional ordering principles retreat, a world of doubles all the more identical for assuming their autonomy, all the more racked by guilt for declaring their emancipation from every law: 'God is dead, so everything is permitted.' 'Nothing is permitted anymore' (Borch-Jacobsen, 1991, p. 129).

This echoes our discussion above on the emergence of the archaic superego, where the criminal and the cop, double and interchange. In the free-market of feelings emerge hate crimes, metonymies of hate, searching at random on the streets for one hate object after another. The archaic superego becomes an undercover double-agent infiltrating the criminal underworld, death squad, the masked hit man, the contract killer to 'take out' what is already dead. Criminal means justify criminal ends. The war on terror becomes terroristic.

The father was the shield against death. In that jealous rivalry with the father, hated to death, lies a narrow footbridge thanks to which the son does not feel directly invaded, directly swallowed by the yawning chasm that opens itself to him as pure and simple unmediated confrontation with the anguish of death. Indeed, the death of the father, whenever it occurs, is felt by the son as a hole that opens in the Real, the radical loss of the bar against the absolute Master — death.

Lacan was quite aware that, in contemporary life, the Symbolic register was more of a structuring mythology than a reality, that underscores some of our preoccupations here, namely, the crisis of the Symbolic, the deficiency of the paternal function, the foreclosure of the Name-of-the-Father, the undermining of the Law, the loss of familial landmarks, and so on. It becomes impossible to separate the Symbolic from the so-called Imaginary identification. Thus to try to appeal to a 'symbolic Law', so obviously obsolete, must have been understood by Lacan as a sort of analytic myth intended to serve as a prop for an onto-ethics of human desire. As Borch-Jacobsen states, 'The Lacanian Oedipus is not the Oedipus as it is; it is the Oedipus as it must be' (Borch-Jacobsen, 1991, p. 226).

But far from the dead father, or the symbolic father, we see another development, the emergence of the *obscene* father. No longer the dead, austere, spiritual, authoritarian, distant father, marginalised long ago by the idealised mother, but the exposure and derailment of this tottering figure by his obscene counterpart. The father, as lewd, lustful, pornographic − not as the intruder who comes between mother and child to initiate differentiation − but the intruder who comes *onto and into* the child. Once the father was feared for his trenchant embodiment of the Law, now, in a reversal, he becomes a terrifying figure. It is not so much that someone breaks the law that disturbs us, but him − the one, above all, who was to be trusted and who was to act as our guarantor.

The father has suddenly come alive! Zizek has it:

> [The] postmodern shift affects radically the status of paternal authority: modernism endeavours to assert the subversive potential of the margins which undermine the Father's authority, of the enjoyments that elude the father's grasp, whereas postmodernism *focuses on the father himself and conceives him as 'alive', in his obscene dimension*.

This strikes terror, because:

> What emerges under the phantom-like 'living dead' − of the spectre which hinders 'normal' sexual relationship − is, however, the reverse of the Name-of-the-Father, namely the 'anal father' who definitely *does enjoy*; the obscene little man who is the clearest embodiment of the phenomenon of the 'uncanny' (*unheimliche*) (Zizek, 1992, pp. 124–5).

This other side of the Name-of-the-Father begins to be revealed historically, Zizek tells us, in Conrad's novels, in the figures of Kurtz in *Heart of Darkness*, and Mister Brown in *Lord Jim*. Marlow encounters Kurtz deep in the midst of the African jungle. Kurtz is a paternal figure who is a master of enjoyment without restraint, a representation of radical evil, all powerful, cruel to the utmost, an absolute Master for whom there are no limits. Yet he is a father who knows beyond the dead neutrality of the Law, a knowledge that is to do with absolute destruction/pleasure of the law beyond the law. This is the father, who lies behind the stabilising father — the warlords, the drug barons, narco-capitalists, tribal chieftains, mercenaries, paramilitaries, terrorists who, a century later, boast of their raping, torturing, ethnic cleansing and casual enjoyment of killing in excess.

With the final postmodern destabilisation of the Symbolic emerges the horror of the obscene father. The agency that was supposed to protect us from the Real, and guarantee some semblance of stability to our world, has finally broken down. With the father moved off his pedestal, exposed as animal, the whole illusion of a stable human reality (underpinned by the Other) has collapsed.

There is widespread disgust at what real fathers might now do, or might indeed have done in the past had we the wit to find out. Currently, there is an orgy of exposing him to ridicule, relentlessly assaulting his potency, the glorious spectacle of his ruin. Grandfathers are accused by their granddaughters, nieces by their uncles; fathers won't bath their daughters. Priests are uncovered as child-abusers. Doctors, teachers, scout leaders, youth leaders, swimming coaches, trainers, etc., are all caught up in this excitement. Whole communities are traumatised (Orkneys, Cleveland). Our masters are exposed, degraded: Freud, the addict and the misogynist; Newton the schizoid; Heidegger the Nazi; Marx the bourgeois; Einstein the clerk; Eliot the obsessionally cold. All mastery neutralised in the name of some murderous obscene 'truth' that will reduce everything to anal indifference, the smearing of the world. The ideological purity of this postmodern crusade, this Inquisition of gentlewomen against fathers, against men, is virulently driven by an envy that would reduce all substance to faeces. Any man, we are told, could be an abuser. Ideology allows for no remainders, therefore all men are implicated. The imaginary symmetrical world of gender rancour is complete. With no third (the symbolic) to mediate, the scene is devastated by mutual projections — immediate, violent and tyrannical.

New Skills, Greater Performance

'Relationships', we must use this word carefully and ironically, are a relatively new concern born with therapy culture. Up until recently families were an extended *economic* unit largely rural, held together (happily or unhappily, this was of no concern) by many cohesive forces. Now, with each member of the unit economically and sexually independent (even the children) the family is required to be and to function as an emotionally gratifying experience, or it is nothing. Nothing holds it together except love. According to Giddens: '"Coupling" and "uncoupling" now provide a more accurate description of the arena of personal life than do "marriage and the family".' A more important question for us than 'Are you married?' is, 'How good is your relationship?'[9] Whereas marriage was a public commitment made in the symbolic register, relationships are fluid, changing, privatised, ephemeral, to be located in the imaginary register.

The key, we are told, is 'emotional literacy' and the capacity for intimacy. Now, all that stands between us and the bleakness of the universe is nothing other than our skills at holding, developing and above all 'negotiating' relationships. Everything is skills based, part of the success of human relations training, which since the 1960s has been driven by global requirements: the need for total mobility, interactivity and communicability within the large corporations and across continents. Untroubled by depth or essence, people are freed-up for continuous re-training and re-skilling in every sphere, carried out through video and IT, the smart end of therapy culture. Women and children are felt to be the most susceptible and willing participants in this new learning. Not only has the personal become political, but the personal becomes instrumental. Our most private affairs must be regulated by the market and run on therapeutic principles.

Children brought up in traditionally domesticated settings are now at a disadvantage with their ongoing propensity for stability, privacy, permanence, anxiety and bondedness. They will lack the necessary flexibility, adaptability and the cool indifference demanded by the system. One can no longer figure the paradoxical labyrinth of postmodernity and it is uncool to try. Instead, learn to *use* the system, the codes, understand the language and, above all, *enjoy*! Be an insider, forget content, focus on form, strategy, profitability, lifestyle options, learn to read the signs. Analysis and interpretation are irrelevant, part of a long-gone metaphysics, a foundational view, an ontological perspective.

Consequently, it no longer makes sense to speak of living together in any simple, permanent or committed sense. 'Relationships' have become highly self-conscious, knowledge/skills/performance based, legalistic, transparent, accountable operations. They are the explosive centre from which all the foreclosed problems of postmodernity continuously threaten to erupt. Hence the need for intensive, proliferating, ongoing skills training on techniques of involvement and intimacy which maximise pleasure and eliminate pain. Sexual relationships are made to bear the brunt of the impossible clash between performance related love, on the one hand, and the violent real of personal abjection, on the other, at a time when they are least supported by any enduring social fabric. Or, put another way, too much craving for love and affection will be channelled into the sexual relationship, the couple, at just the time when such relationships have become most problematic in their shallowness and ephemerality. A vicious circle is set up, a kind of ultimately uninhabitable sexual ghetto is created: I *demand* you to love me (I claim I didn't have it as a child, and I can't get it from anywhere else). I cannot stand your demand, not least because I have the same demands of my own that I want *you* to gratify. Fuck you if you won't love me. Yes. And fuck you too. Rejection gratifies the archaic super-ego, but simultaneously increases demand.

Legalistic frameworks and guidelines now surround all types of relationships to guard against the possibilities of abuse, harassment, discrimination, intimidation, exploitation and so on, all testifying to the absolute presence (unrepressed, yet split-off and not really felt) of unassimilable pain. Notions of social and sexual hygiene and security pervade contemporary life. Insurance against death, sudden accident, serious illness, job-loss, protection policies, personal alarms, alarms at home, at work, in the car, all screeching and screaming at us *from the outside. We must be secure.* Your happiness depends on your security. Our communicational skills, our sexual and behavioural classes, our therapy, these labours of love and perfection, are designed to close off all the cracks and wrinkles, the signs of death. The intense work we do to pursue our own sexual and economic freedoms has made the pain of life unbearable.

What are left are *model* relationships — relationships as image, hollowed out from the inside, as it were, while no one was noticing. Everything looks the same, but everything has gone. The missing depth is matched by the brilliance of the image. The real of relationship is replaced by fabrication and performance. The sacrament of marriage, which only 30 years ago it was considered a crime to break up, has been replaced by limited contracts and faultless pain-free separation. Marriage has become what Giddens calls one of the 'shell institutions'. There is now no shame or loss attached to marriage break-down, only the potential shame and social ostracism of not *managing* it effectively through therapy (so that you can remain friends, for the sake of the children). Now, the social stigma might well be your *refusal* to accept loss and change, of *remaining* married and thus burying your potential. Those who do remain married, fearing their minority status, should be in therapy to find out what they are doing wrong. The anxiety around staying together and missing out is increasing all the time, just like the anxiety of being too heterosexual — you must be homophobic. Attachment behaviour is a crime against freedom, resisting the natural rhythm of the coupling/uncoupling cycle. Did you ever think you may be co-dependent, trapped by guilt into being with your partner? Therapy becomes the mass management of break-up and pain — commiseration.

A process has accelerated in the last 30 years in which what we might call a huge negative space has opened up within what was formerly a great religious and secular tradition of faith. This loss of faith in the great ideologies, has led to what the Mexican poet, Octavio Paz, noted as the appearance of 'the ghosts of religion'. 'The emptiness can be filled with caricatures such as communism or fascism or total ideas, or with sects, all this flowering of superstitious selves in the Western world' (Paz, 1986, p. 18). Into this negative space, come animal rights, fundamentalisms of all kinds, eco-terrorism, new age philosophies, and, above all, therapy. These are not moral commitments in any old sense, which always allowed space for the immoral, amoral or the irreligious, but rather paranoid domains of *pure* meaning, unsullied, uncomplicated and requiring no personal sacrifice. These new extremist cults threaten to mop up the free-floating moral energy generated by the entropy of capitalism in its virulent post-Marxist phase, and parallels what Baudrillard has called the more generalised 'terroristic fundamentalism of this new sacrificial religion of *performance*' (Baudrillard, 1992, pp. 106–7; emphasis added).

It will be to our performance that we must continuously sacrifice ourselves. Getting the very best out of people (of oneself), at work, at leisure, at sport, at sex, what we all experience as tougher, leaner, thinner lives, hidden only thinly by the promise, for the few, of economic advancement, the injunction is — *perform or die*. What Thatcher and then the new Right have done is concentrated the mind and removed once and for all the subversive transitional space, and replaced it with intimidation, extortion and protectionism. Everything is simplified: perform *and* die.[10]

Morality is linked to the superego, whereas perfection is linked to the ideal ego. Freud noted that, 'This ideal ego is now the target of the self-love which was enjoyed in childhood by the actual ego. The subject's narcissism makes its appearance displaced onto this new ideal ego, which like the infantile ego, finds itself possessed of every perfection that is of value' (Freud, 1914, p. 94). Unlike the superego that lacks and is there to be challenged and rebelled against, the ideal ego is *total* and makes impossible demands in the pursuit of its happiness. The ideal is linked with the mother, with the *desire-of-the-mother*. Lacan and Klein have pointed to the horror of this ideal double that threatens death.

On the contrary, we now believe that the perfect and most sublime form of love is the love of self. Disappointed by the incredible work of perfection required at the hetero- and even the homosexual levels, the self offers itself as the perfect object of desire. Self-caress, which is everywhere commercialised in creams, oils, shampoos, medicaments, massage therapies, extends globally on the internet as virtual sex. The net has revived the old pleasures of masturbation and facilitated the development of a 'pornocracy', the inalienable right of each to their own sexual process, which can now be minutely and exquisitely controlled and prolonged by the mouse. Marcuse, following Eisenhower, spoke of the Military Industrial Complex. Now, post-industrially information technology is driven by the sexual military, that vast army of sexual dealers, innovators, entrepreneurs, pimps and sex slaves dedicated to the exploitation of every solitary niche of the virtual and its world-wide deployment, as the real of eroticism like the real of the world becomes its own false memory.

But there may still be hope. There are pockets of conviviality, congeniality and friendliness. Perhaps a parallel universe exists, unknown and unseen and therefore incapable of degradation by representation. This is part of the stubbornly persistent real of the social, paradoxically beyond and yet always present. It is the immediacy of the encounter, the spark, the light, the instant before words, lost without trace as soon as we speak. It cannot form the basis of a relationship because it is totally ephemeral, but no relationship has any liveliness at all without participation in this real. Neither is it a transitional space. Once it is named it is trapped and lost. It is not part of any mental apparatus, conscious or unconscious, and therefore it is not part of psychoanalysis, and yet any psychotherapeutic process would be dead without it. It is what is cynically evoked in commercials that use rural idylls, landscapes, children talking, etc., only to perish instantly on contact with this real. In the increasingly extreme conditions of our culture in the West, less and less of this liveliness can infuse relationships, because the space (free, neutral, secret, transitional) required has been booked, double-booked *in advance*. The crucial question now is whether or not this is indeed an irreversible process.

Notes

1. The use of the term Oedipus, Oedipus Complex, etc., throughout is not meant to be taken literally or developmentally in this context. I am using the term in its Lacanian sense, as a *structuring* phenomenon, by which human desire becomes possible. In this sense, the term does not only refer to the modern Western nuclear family, and the two movements referred to are not necessarily carried out by a biological mother and a father.

2. Currently, Ireland is painfully coming to terms with rural and urban child neglect. Childcare workers, parents, the Religious and the state are being rigorously held to account for the brutal treatment of children in schools, homes, orphanages, and industrial schools during the middle of the last century. Public confessions, apologies and compensation are demanded by the victims. Few concessions are made and little account is taken of the poverty of families, the almost total lack of state finance and training during that era when children were objects, chattels, slaves to their masters. The ideological assumption is that now, *we* are correct. No account is taken of the

possibility that level three may yet constitute new extravagant forms of abuse by excess — children who are feral at home. You mean to say that you let children isolate themselves in their rooms with television, video, sound systems, DVD and the net, and you let them have whatever they wanted, so that you could be free!

3. This polarisation is somewhat unfair. Winnicott and others (the British Independents) were of course aware that children were far from innocent. But they did privilege the innate capacity, given good enough mothering, for spontaneity, concern and creativity. They have been frequently criticised for their emphasis on the mother.

4. This breakdown and loss is real and is increasing. Against the criticism that this assertion is merely part of a modern moral panic and nostalgia, or so-called 'golden-age-ism', we should cite, for instance, British Home Offices figures that show a sevenfold increase in reported violent crime within a generation, and a massive 40% increase during the 1980s. People who live in poor areas are seven times more likely to suffer from violent crime than those in more prosperous middle-class areas. On the other hand, we are not asserting that the 1950s or any other period (e.g. the late Victorian period) was necessarily 'better' in any simplistic sense, or that there was ever any golden age to which we might return. However, the decline is no longer localised in poor or disadvantaged areas. Furthermore, *this* decline is unique as it takes place within the context of a radical moral indeterminacy.

5. Psychoanalysis makes abundantly clear that the self and its stability is not in any sense pre-given or automatic. The self is a social construct. It has to be formed within a social milieu, which involves deep, reliable and sustained contact with significant others over a long period. What happens on the microsocial level and what is deemed essential for emotional stability is what, for instance, Bion calls 'reverie' and what Winnicott calls 'environmental provision' or 'holding'.

6. Before sex was 'liberated' it made no sense to talk of sexual 'crimes' as what we now call sex was part of the dark margin of the obscene — quite literally off the scene.

7. This 'end' is paradoxical. Psychoanalysis is about the unconscious, but if this is exposed as our (modern) myth, if it becomes simply irrelevant or unnecessary, or if it is simply 'liberated' or overthrown, where does this leave psychoanalysis? This is where Lacan becomes important with his dogmatic assertion that the unconscious persists and insists as a kernel of radical otherness and difference. But this may be wishful thinking.

8. The maternal feminine has nothing specifically to do with women or with mothers, but refers to an underlying imaginary principle of benign Being, beyond culture, the law, beyond anything that we might say or do in the differentiated world of the Symbolic. In this reaction, against patriarchy, Being is invoked erroneously as a consolation.

9. A. Giddens. *1999 Reith Lectures*. Lecture 4, p. 4.

10. The current devastating loss of what Lacan refers to as 'ratification' or 'assent' of the child's image of itself in the mirror, its acknowledgement or registration by the Symbolic, which no longer exists in its strong form, leads the child to an absolute impasse. All that is left are the frenetic attempts to gain authorisation by the Imaginary. My personal best is not good enough and never will be. There is no limit. However well I perform for the imaginary other, I am nothing, I am illegitimate.

Chapter 4

Psychoanalysis & Postmodernity

As she lay there, laughing, the traveller hurried forward to give comfort. And the comfort was intolerable to her. Two strokes of the hair, soft words, a helping hand: this was what made the woman cry. The present seemed perfectly bearable – indeed, hilarious – until you felt again what it was like when people were kind. Then the present was bearable no longer. So the old woman wept. So the blind man wept. They can take it so long as no one is kind. – Amis (1982), p. 222

The Transition

For most academic authors the transition from modernity to what we often call postmodernity occurs during the 1960s or 1970s. Charles Jencks marks a specific moment for that transition, in 1972 when, in architecture at least, modern buildings and housing complexes, designed for compliant and happy workers, were demolished, blown up on a large scale, in reaction to the hegemony of high scientific modernism: 'This explosion of 1972, copied countless times throughout the world as a radical way of dealing with such housing estates, soon came to symbolise the mythical death of *modern* architecture' (Jencks, 1992, p. 24). This was the end of modernism as a project.

There are a number of linked terms: postmodernism, post-structuralism, post-industrial, all connoting something 'post', something different, ending, all implying a paradigm shift or rupture which, I shall argue here specifically in relation to that great modern idea psychoanalysis, has precipitated us into what Baudrillard (1992) refers to as 'a process of systematic obliteration', or Jameson's (1991) 'schizophrenic disjunction' fragmentation, and 'a rubble of distinct and unrelated signifiers' (p. 26). Or, take Young's (1989) assertion, 'the post-modern seems to me to pronounce the jaded to be all we can have' (p. 87). Or, Lyotard's (1979), 'incredulity towards metanarratives' (p. xxiv) or Hebdige's (1988) celebration of the 'end of all (oppressive) powers' (p. 196) or Eagleton's ironic comment on the end of alienation: 'There is no longer any subject to be alienated from, "authenticity" having been less rejected than merely forgotten' (cited in Jencks, 1992, p. 132). Ihab Hussan (1992) notes ominously, 'Everywhere now we observe societies riven by the double and coeval process of planetisation and retribalisation, totalitarianism and terror, fanatic faith and radical disbelief. Everywhere we meet, in mutant or displaced forms, that conjunctive/disjunctive technological rage which affects postmodern discourse' (p. 204).

Whatever the problematic value of historical categorisations — pre-modern, modern, postmodern, late modern, one thing is clear: the contemporary has become radical, extreme and violent.

Baudrillard says: 'Now everything has been liberated, the chips are down, and we find ourselves collectively faced with the big question: WHAT DO WE DO NOW THE ORGY IS OVER?' (Baudrillard, 1990, p. 3; capitalisation in the original). Now, we can only hyper-realise these events as though they had not been in what becomes an endless déjà vu of postmodernity. The process of modernity has run its course — all traditional (pre-modern) structures have been challenged and exposed, uprooted, raised, in the ecstatic shock of the new. 'Making it all anew' was the slogan of the modernism. In its turn, classical high modernism itself became the new canon and the new authority to be stripped bare, torn down, demystified. Entry to the fractal zone: Lyotard's notion of clouds of linguistic particles, or floating signifiers in which we are all bathed, circulating around us in a storm of commercialisation, of minutely differentiated commodities, as consumerism overdrives itself for the whole world, for global enjoyment. Capitalism is the ubiquitous engine of postmodernity — capitalism in its third form, its most cannibalistic form — that eats tradition, eats referents, brings about ecstatic randomness, dazzling dispersions of everything that former generations once believed in.

Against Baudrillard, orgy is just beginning. Enclaves of traditionalism, in pockets in the third world, or the third world in the first world, to be precipitated (liberated from poverty) into postmodernity, without the intermediary stages that have made the process tolerable for the first world, for us, hiding its worst excesses. *We* have sustained the long process of softening up which has hidden our helplessness, irrelevance and stupidity, under the guise of empowerment and choice. Some still believe that we can modify a process that has now become global — *trans*-everything — transnational, transeconomic, transpolitical, transcultural, transgenic. It is impossible to describe this aleatory process or represent it in any way, except by extremes. Reason hurries to catch up with what is fundamentally irrational, demonic. Reason, especially therapeutic reason, tries to extend itself with all its goodness, understanding and fairness into the alien sphere of complete turbulence.

Psychoanalysis

Where does this leave our work as psychoanalysts? This is almost a trivial question in the immensity of the hyperreal, where the so-called 'death of the subject' has become a cliché, is so common-place, it no longer rouses more than a flicker of interest or complaint. Psychoanalysis was discovered at the high point of modernity, and it contains within itself a fundamental paradox, between Freud *one* and Freud *two*.[1] This paradox mirrors modernity itself. On the one hand, the decentring of all tradition, and on the other the assertion of the authority of the transcendent ego. Spanning this paradox, psy-choanalytic therapy takes place in a reliable setting — the containing environment of Bion, or the holding environment of Winnicott, rep-resented by the consulting room, a safe enclosure, a safe haven for the ego for the elaboration of a personal style or idiom *in the midst of anxiety*. Anxiety? Yes, anxiety — a concern that slipped out with modernity itself.

What about psychoanalysis, now, where only text counts, where the subject fades or is no one, and no one remembers when it was someone? When the unconscious has been transpired, when sex is performative and cool, when Melanie Klein's visceral descriptions of primitive phantasies can be seen on adult movie channels, or the global pornography net,[2] what more is there after the orgy? Should psychoanalysis itself become postmodern? Lacan has pushed this, *not* responding, *not* knowing, being otherwise, signifiers not signifieds, interrogation, deconstruction, punctuation, etc. Now, a realistic, tougher psychoanalysis for the postmodern subject, tearing into the mother's room upsetting the infant being nurtured there. No more (modernist) illusions, except 'good speaking!', however ironic that must now seem. Why not abandon the consulting room alto-gether, conduct analyses in places that are emblematic of post-modernity itself — in the airport terminal, the lobby of an interconti-nental hotel, the hard shoulder of the transcontinental highway, the out of town shopping precinct, the multi-story car park, cyberspace?

Non-places, emptied places, part of hyperspace, mediate contem-porary life — molecular, cellular, promiscuously plural, trafficking in disaffected persons. Belonging to no one, cared about by no one, except in a technical sense (by signs welcoming us, thanking-us, etc.), these spaces are fabricated, utilitarian, depersonalised. The underneaths of motorway bridges, ruined inner city areas, like empty atomic orbitals, may occasionally be occupied by migrants or nomads — the sub-atomic particles of the underclass, subjects without bearings, co-ordinates, referents. People, the corralled, the get-in-lane people, each is truly an orphan of the system which adopts him with love. The subject encounters the last frontier, death itself, the total absence of the familiar. Hyperspace familiarises us with the cold of the universe without life, promoting electronic, digital friendliness, welcoming, always a flashing neon parody of hospitality.

We don't have to go this far, the postmodern patient is but one step away from cool hyperspace itself. The derealised self, impinged upon, no longer there, needs not *more* impingement, but some minimal care, which psychoanalysis offers in all its forms. Anymore than in Freud's day, we cannot ignore the wider culture, what effect does it have, firstly on patients, and secondly on the analytic approach? Can we still proceed broadly in the same way that Freud did, with everything still in place, but changing? Does Winnicott's elegy of the stable family still hold, 'with the mother happy in her marriage, and with the father ready to play his part with the children?' (Winnicott, 1987, p. 85). Or, should we count any longer on a residual capacity to be alone, resulting from, 'the early experience of being alone in the presence of someone' (Winnicott, 1958, p. 32). Now: the permanent experience of being alone in the presence of everyone; the mother happy to be out of her marriage (often either in therapy or doing therapy or both) and the father happy to be a mother. Can we seriously believe that the subject may become autonomous through a therapeutic process, when a belief in autonomy died with the death of the modern itself, and when the notion of a self, an identity, is exposed as flawed? Can we, indeed, be optimistic, that in the exploded fragments of high Western culture, the postmodern subject can (for the first time) ironically really become answerable and free — free from commitments, tradition and belief? Or, is it more likely that the subject has disappeared into a promiscuous sign system, texting, clicking and surfing? *Drowning not waving.*

Critical Distance

If modernism was the age of anxiety, alienation and abstraction, it has been re-read as the *post*-modern *jouissance* of lack, absence, traces, *differance*, multiple-coding. Modernism equalled bourgeois liberalism, *personal* style, positivism and humanism. Modernism was also an 'International Style' in architecture, with its cultural transcendence, universal grammar, acontextuality, oppositional voice, now exploded by the postmodern return to the vernacular. Modernist notions have been displaced by, or may still co-exist with:

1) the collapse of inner and outer imperialisms — collapse of *mastery*, in all its forms;

2) the impact of feminism;

3) the awareness of the ecological movement;

4) openness to non-European cultures;

5) liberation theology and ecumenism;

6) the conflation of 'high' culture with 'pop' culture and mass commercialisation of all forms — commodity aesthetics;

7) new holistic science;

8) our fascination with and captivation by electronic multimedia; and finally and fatally,

9) the rise of fundamentalisms.

Terry Eagleton argues for critical perspective. A critique that establishes 'an implacable distance between itself and the social order'. This is not yet the end of subjectivity. The situation is complex. He compromises: 'The subject of late capitalism is neither simply the self-regulating synthetic agent [ego/self] posited by classical humanist ideology, nor simply a decentred network of desire [split subject, drowning, etc.], but a contradictory amalgam of the two' (cited in Jencks, 1992, pp. 114–15). The problem is to find a place 'outside', when there is no longer any outside, no place left not colonised *in advance*. We can no longer speak innocently — that is *outside* of some ideological language. There is no meta-authority, no ultimate truth.[3] Orwell's prediction has come true: 'The very concept of objective truth is fading out of the world' (Orwell, 1961, p. 212).

Critical theory faces the formidable task of unveiling structures of domination when no one is dominating, nothing is being dominated and grounds no longer exist for the old principle of liberation from domination. Domination has been replaced by the therapeutic management of 'needs'. Try to criticise therapeutic reason. You will be told you need help like the Russian dissidents required to have psychiatric treatment. Or you might need a 'corrective emotional experience', a chance to develop 'healthy behaviours', or 'improved cognitive functioning.' Therapeutic reason reaches corners that other ideologies fail to reach. It disarms all previous positions and therefore has a global reach.

The resulting collapse of critical faith in a self-determining position is, according to Toynbee, in his very influential *A Study of History*, the precursor to the breakdown of civilisations, the point at which human beings lose control over their own destinies, which he felt was due to some fundamental moral aberration. In a similar vein, George Steiner commented in a television programme on what he called 'the fate of ultimate values in this century of barbarism. Without a belief in God, with words rendered meaningless by deconstruction and nihilism, neither art nor human values can survive.' In his book *Real Presences,* Steiner predicts: 'What I affirm is the intuition that where God's presence is no longer a tenable supposition and where His absence is no longer a felt, indeed overwhelming weight, certain [critical] dimensions of thought and creativity are no longer attainable' (Steiner, 1989, p. 229). Indeed, His *absence* is widely felt to be liberating, especially in therapeutic circles. However, he *can* return, but only in his weightless form as a spiritual adjunct to narcissistic consumption: God speaks to me in my human nature, my sexuality, etc. God's absolute density has been sold off, privatised and deregulated in the West.

The West has taken therapeutic tolerance to the point of cultural suicide.[4] For a long time, accused of dominating the world with its technological materialism, the West, full of guilt, has become alien to itself and vulnerable to every influence without critical judgement. Anyone can walk right in: to our computer systems and crash them; to a public space with a bomb (my right to bomb you); to your religion and secularise it; to your family and take away the father; to your politics and globalise everything; to your free speech and impose a *Fatwah*. Even at the level of the body: walk right into your immune system and take your T-lymphocytes and with them the capacity to resist even low grade infections. The West is criminal openness and relativity, paralysed by multiplicity, no resistance is offered. That was until 9/11.

1950s and Now

The postmodern period is criss-crossed by impossible contradictions and multiple-codings. When we compare the 1950s to now, we get some measure of the immense changes involved. The 1950s saw the post-war emphasis on renewal, the health service, health for all, stability, the rapidly increasing wealth of the middle classes, and the beginning of the end of working class proletarian politics. There were new consumer durables, and this was the beginning of the long slow 'exit from politics'. There was relative integration of the super-ego structures of church, school, police, family. After the catastrophe, the total destruction of war, there was the work of rebuilding, reforming, restructuring. Teaching, for instance, the peasants of the third world that, in the words of scientists at the time, 'you will have to change your traditional ways — grow the new genetically enhanced crop varieties, borrow the money to buy the agri-chemicals, inoculate your children, plan your families, etc.' Control was through science, centralisation, corporate expansion, the paradigm was modernist universalism. According to Hobsbawm, for 80% of humanity, the Middle Ages ended suddenly in the 1950s.

As an adolescent, I could divide my father's friends who fought in the war into two unequal groups: the largest by far was the group that made no comment at all, or, made light of it and spoke often enough about having had a 'good war'. The other group would privately acknowledge the *unforgettable* nature of what they had been through and what they had seen. I wondered even then how would they ever be able to endure the trivialisation of everything[5] — *this is what we fought for*? The new supermarkets, the family saloon, refrigeration, TV, home movies, the wireless, a new-found confident bourgeois nuclear respectability of a very conservative kind, and the slow transpiration of collective values in the face of burgeoning and increasingly privatised mass consumption, the exponential growth of which, in the 1980s and 1990s was to have a more radicalising effect than any Leftist politics.

In David Lynch's film *Blue Velvet*, American small town provincial life complete with good college teenage couple uncover a (brutal) hidden reality of drugs and sadomasochism represented in the first instance by the shocking apparition of a severed ear in the grass, a close up shows it to be crawling with ants. The storyline is complete when the hero rescues the woman, kills her torturer and marries his college sweetheart. What is interesting about this film is that it catches us *between* two images: of the wholesomely good 1950s; and the vicious but ultimately silly stereotype of a perverse drug culture. Two images are juxtaposed, yet are eaten away all the while from the inside by the insects.

As Zizec says in relation to the fundamental ambiguity of the image in contemporary culture, 'it is a kind of barrier enabling the subject to maintain distance from the Real, protecting him/her against its inruption, yet its very obtrusive "hyperrealism" evokes the nausea of the Real' (Zizek, 1992, pp. 129–30).

One of the contemporary's many starting points, in the 1950s: the barrier against the Real met its ideal in the retrenchment offered by the suburban set-up with the garden and nuclear family — the invented intermediary between the Real of the city and the rural. The suburban was in the vanguard of political minimalism, with its cathexis of the garden centre, the golf club, the pub, the superstore.

What was decathected was the public space. Before the war, the life of the market, the street, parks, pubs, football, cinema, politics, courting, even television at first, were all done in the public arena.

Creeping privatisation was the beginning of the end of the social, and all capital to do with the collective. What took its place was the universalisation of the image, the colonisation of the public *and* the private by the towering ascendancy of the burgeoning mass- media creating the hyperreal. Each of us in time was obliged to become expert interactive media technicians. Isolated not only from the community and the public sphere, but now passively confined to our own rooms in front of a screen.

The mediated hyperreal steels the public space of the community. The real has been purloined by the hyper. For instance: hyperactivity replaces the real of paralysing fear; hyperspace negates the loss of bearings and coordinates; hyperkinesis occludes the real inertia and indifference of the masses; hypertension precedes the attack on the heart of reality. The hyperreal will shine out brilliantly when all other inferior life forms have long since died.

Modernism was modernism when there were still premodern enclaves to be colonised: peasants subsisting alongside automated factories; wildlife at the edges of ribbon prairie monocultures; aboriginal tribes watching MTV, and so on. This violent process, on the way to completion, becomes the postmodern, when it makes no sense any longer to speak of 'breaking new ground'. Instead, we are left to pick over the traces, appropriating, cannibalising, recycling bits of the past.

The hegemony of the universal scientific ultra-rationalist approach was to implode with uncertainty, chaos and complexity. A whole marginalised world was discovered beyond centralised control — unpredictability, instability, non-linearity. We moved from a confident position of control in the 1950s and 1960s, to 'management' in 1980s and 1990s, reduced to the monitoring of catastrophic systems. The 500 year domination by Europe was over. Mastery no more. Or rather, the margin is the master; every margin wants to become master in her own right. With therapeutic empowerment: be your own master!

Radical Discontinuities

The subtle masters of the world are tourism and therapy. Tourism is postmodern: a creeping prostitution. The world is made to give herself, make herself available without commitment or protest, for abundant play time. Tourism, the legitimisation of the violating appropriation of strangeness, forces the other out of her alterity, to smile, dance and give whatever services are required to the curb crawlers of the world.

Therapy is tourism on the *inside*. The inner tourist like his outer counterpart feels obliged to visit every psychic site (the collective unconscious, the personal unconscious, the dream, the soul, past souls, the fantasy, the archetypes, the birth experience, before birth experience, etc.) believing that by doing so he will improve himself. Just like the outer, the inner sites offer themselves on the secret condition that nothing real is given. This nauseating lack of the Real forces more and more touristic and therapeutic activity. Trudging around the planet, tourists create archaeological waste objects to support a fantasy of self-improvement. Similarly therapy violates the soul, plundering its reserves without restraint. Tourism and therapy empty the worlds they pretend to be interested in.

There is only the past to look back on nostalgically, the commercial cultivation of traditional rural idylls. Take, for instance, Donegal 'traditional handicrafts', mass-marketed with glossy brochures of how the 'natural' dyes are obtained from the local heathers and lichens — for Italian, Japanese, American coachloads. Donegal peasants, suddenly transformed into cute-whore executives (in aircraft hanger sized retail outlets in the middle of the bog and the drizzle), are on-hand and will be pleased to answer any of your questions (in any language). The unselfconscious natural grace and toughness of the Donegal people enters the global economy, in an aggressive simulated form, as a marketable commodity.

The black ultra cool automobile alone on a road in an Australian desert, parked near an aboriginal boy undergoing his initiation, almost naked, spearing a wild animal. Or, Catholic nuns, on their way from prayers, descending the cathedral steps, discuss in hushed tones the sexiness of IBM software — 'really hot!' Contemplative monks jump and scream for joy at winning the Lotto.

Radical discontinuity, confusion, abolition of historical sense, and the reinvention of authenticity: coffee, instant coffee, decaf, then *real* coffee. 'Real' like its counterparts 'natural' or 'organic' is appended to sell products, such is our hunger for authenticity. A more sinister note was struck in Wales, where the slogan was, 'Come home to a real fire' as the Nationalists set about torching holiday homes.

Baudrillard notes that they are building an opera house at the Bastille. 'The people will no longer have to storm it, they will go there to feast on regal music. Actually the people will not go now — the cultivated people will go, and in so doing will provide a stunning confirmation of the rule that the privileged are always ready to sanctify through art or pleasure the sites where others have fought' (Baudrillard, 1980–85, p. 186).

An ad on Dublin radio invites us to '*Get to the GPO!*', not any longer to die hopelessly fighting the British at the height of their Imperial power in 1916, but, you fool, 'Get to the *new* GPO shopping arcade, shopping extravaganza, with bargains galore'.

In the early 1980s, death squads in El Salvador attacked and killed 'hundreds of Leftists a week'. But, says our Salvadorian commentator, cheerily:

> One sign that our country has put its dark past behind us can be found at the Puertas del Diablo, or 'Devil Doors', two huge rock formations on the volcanoes above San Salvador. Right-wing death squads once used the site as a favourite dumping ground for corpses. It's now a favourite picnic site.

Why not?

And why not a Belfast 'Troubles tour'? There's now more to Belfast than shopping. Belfast Citybus has introduced, to its Living History Tour, new sites, which according to the organisers are oversubscribed. Visit Penny Lane opposite Casement Park where two British army corporals were stripped then murdered by the IRA. Visit the gap where Frizzell's Fish Shop was before the Shankill bomb. Visits to all the dead sites of living history.

Down in County Kerry, visit the Muckross Traditional Farmhouses, 'where the daily life of a old rural farming community is portrayed on real working farms complete with farm animals, etc. It provides a fascinating contrast to the lifestyle of the gentry, which you have just seen in Muckross House. Thank you for visiting. Have a safe journey home'.

Apropos, the fiftieth anniversary of the D-day landings in 1994, a holiday and travel programme ran the following commercial. Thinking of travelling to the continent this summer? If you are a D-day veteran travelling with us, we would like you to celebrate with us with a free bottle of Calvados.

We have 'Vietnam Season' on television. And in North Vietnam itself, at Cu Chi, tourists can explore the underground passageways built by the Vietcong which helped them finally win the war against their most murderous aggressor of all. The tunnels, at one time small, cramped, fetid, wet and crawling with insects, have been greatly enlarged and cleaned up so that even the most obese Westerners can get through with their camcorders intact, and they are led by bright, young Vietnamese men and women, dressed in the original fatigues of the Vietcong. At the end of the tour, there is a shooting competition, in which, if you score a direct hit, you will win a traditional Vietcong black and white scarf. Entertainment on the back of an extraordinary sacrifice.

The erasure of historical referents, and the constant recycling in museums, heritage parks, and the like, *must be fun*, fun for all the family. Eco indicates that, 'The frantic desire for the Almost Real arises as a neurotic reaction to the vacuum of memories; the Absolute Fake is the offspring of the unhappy awareness of a present without depth' (Eco, 1973, pp. 30–1). But above all, there is overwhelming obligation to be entertaining, with no flicker of irony, no trace of this 'unhappy awareness', except a kind of bingeing on multimedia displays.

Just as the classical sexual fetish marks the horror of the glimpse of the 'gap' in the female sexual organs, so too heritage fetish objects and their mass proliferation, conceal the aporia which opens up in the artificial potency of the world. This disavowal by the historical fetish, the refusal of the Real as catastrophic, requires a massive expenditure of life, the split consciousness of looking but never seeing.

More of the Same Difference

It is no longer possible to be an outsider. The old existential heroes, the lovers of solitude, the rebels, the prophets, who took space to 'expose' the system, are gone, along with existentialism itself. Oddballs, freaks, misfits are recontextualised as sociological categories, and sub-categories, to be 'managed' by the system.

With the loss of any macropolitical objectives, come proliferations of micropolitical groupings — *groupuscules* (Jameson). Everyone belongs to a group. Each group is politically marked. Each group will claim to have been victimised. Not just the obvious examples, like blacks, gays and women, but also *privileged* groups lay claim to grievance. Many tens of differentiated sub-groupings, more all the time, can make a claim for equality or positive discrimination, irrespective of merit. White Afrikaners feel discriminated against. White racists in Europe feel attacked by the media. In Britain, the host population is another ethnic group fighting for survival in media-space. In the absence of individual thought, there is groupspeak, lobbyists, slogans, propaganda endlessly reiterated through media. Power in suffering.

Since therapy has seen to it that we take ourselves as our object, our chief object of passion, what else can we find but our own desolation and become passionate about that. According to Robert Hughes, 'Only the victim shall be hero' (Hughes, 1993, p. 7). He speaks of the dangers of this massive retreat into the subjective away from politics and the objective, quoting Goethe, 'Epochs which are regressive, and in the process of dissolution, are always subjective, whereas the trend in all progressive epochs is objective . . . Every truly excellent endeavour turns from within towards the world' (p. 10). As all identities are failing by sheer multiplicity, complexity and equalisation: only the worst, the most sacrificial can stand out.

Furthermore, organisations and institutions appear corrupt, riven with dissatisfaction and dissent — virtual narcissisms of small differences. No one can be trusted not to discriminate against you in this new hypersubjective environment, where the only loyalty you should have is to yourself and to your feelings. The huge therapeutic and commercial forces engaged in the promotion and selling of the happy consciousness, customer care, happy hours, personalised service, comfort zones and the like, can never quite close the gap through which pours forth the resentment of everything.

A recent programme focused on gay women. It mounted a strident attack on anyone who might have been half-hearted about lesbian chic. Various women were interviewed, each asserting pride in their homosexuality, their image, difference, sexual practices, right to live together, to adopt children, their grievance against the straight world, etc. All image and potency with barely concealed rancour.

However, much of the current rage and resentment is staged for marketing purposes. Brutality, coarseness, humiliation, pornography: it is ironic, a play of appearances, making *real* disillusion seem uncool. The result is that nothing can be taken seriously, except as part of the market, which deprives the Real of its seriousness in advance. Chill out, do not analyse the 'deep' meanings of our current malaise because to do so is to miss the *play* of reality and difference.

The totallising, rationalising, controlling Western consciousness, celebrating itself as therapeutic and caring, brings racist separatism in its wake. As a result of progressive exclusions (sanitisations) by the humanist conception of man, what Bataille calls 'the accursed share' accumulates on the Other side. Foucault analysed the exclusion of the mad at the dawn of the modern period into the asylums, the confinement of criminals to the prison. There is a whole genealogy of exclusions: the exclusion of children into the school ghetto, the exclusion of women, gays, transsexuals, the disabled, the subnormal, etc. Now, via a therapeutic sleight of hand, you can be part of us again, but *on our terms*, which are the terms of reason, visibility and accountability. *Nothing can be foreign to us.* We must *see* you!

Exposure creates the illusion of difference — tolerable and even mildly interesting, certainly educative — *within the Same*. Otherness, raw Otherness belongs to the *singularity*, the invisible, the unrepresentable, the unfathomable, which becomes, in modernity, a waste product, a residue. The Other must collude with the media, be registered (online), as it were, and be condemned to mere (dis)appearance. So the Other becomes, available, fashionable, prideful, self-promotional, devoid of all mystery and complicity! All mediated disjunctions, differences, neutralise each other in the endless babble of democratic interactivity. Free speech — give us your view after the show. Email us. Say something outrageous! What follows is a vast equivocation of all circuits, a virtual jamming of all ideas, venting under the guise of free access. Nothing counts for nothing.

What nevertheless remains 'outside', as some *unassimilable* excess, radically alien, *cannot* be located in a rational account of difference, however sophisticated and subtle the psychological, cultural, anthropological, moral, the conception of the other appears to be. One should never be fooled by appearances: by generosity, by openness, by simplicity, the genuineness of the people, etc. Having murdered all this at the start, we become nostalgic and fetishistic about ethnicity and moved by the spectacle of our desire to be inclusive after the centuries of exclusion, domination and exploitation! Recognition, Rights, Autonomy, Difference, the drip feed of inclusion, this is how things have been turned around, and victory consolidated. Fundamentally, it is an *economic* victory, the mere *selling* of difference, that no Other can possibly hope to resist. Only the question remains as how best to manage their own disappearance.

Zizec speaks of the 'fantasy' of the harmoniously functioning modern democratic state with all discontinuities, depravities, the antagonisms (Otherness) erased. This collective fantasy has a stabilising effect. However, the destabilising dimension of the fantasy and what it encompasses and hides is productive of racism. Images haunt me about what he or she, of the other race, is doing when *out of my sight*, deceiving or plotting against me, ignoring or indulging in an enjoyment that is more pleasurable, intense or perverted than any I will experience. This enjoyment (*jouissance*) of the Other becomes the focus of my envious preoccupation in an otherwise ideally reconciled liberal state. He is lazy, he is perverse, dirty, etc. and he enjoys being so. Zizec is against the former interpretation of racism as the projection of split-off 'inner conflicts' into the Other. For Zizec, the racist is *always*, '*originally decentred*, part of an opaque network [the Symbolic] whose meaning and logic eludes his control' (Zizec, 1992, p. 195; added emphasis). The Other always has what *I* want, hence my preoccupation with him and *his* enjoyment and the lewd descriptions and demonisations. Indeed I hate him because he is *more* me than I am myself. In this formulation, racism is the return of the exotic, some erotic excess (Bataille), from within the stabilised fabric-ation of modern inclusive democracies. Racism is the Real that supports the illusion of democratic participation and reconciliation. Racism is a persistent sharp focus of repudiation, fascination and violent persecution emerging from the purified, pacified masses secretly wanting to retain a violent murderous bond with the *lost* object, the foreign body of pleasure.

With this Other increasingly 'reconciled' with the Same, occupying the same public and cultural space, the same resources, racism can only grow. It comes from two sides, from the 'host' country mortally fearful of the proximity of his alien object of desire, and from the Other who was originally confined in his 'strangeness' and invisibility. What vehemence, what death drive of exclusion, awaits us in our complacent therapeutic and moral superiority?

What moral educators and therapists believe is progress in acceptance of diversity, barely conceals a corresponding widespread rage of indifference which has no particular object. It could be anything, as exemplified by people we hear of occasionally who are 'allergic to modern living'. They can't drink the water, breathe the air, or eat any kind of food, for fear of a massive anti-allergic response. *Mental* indifference produces reactions at the tissue and organ level. Our culture's decision to include everything, to reconcile everything, creates massive overcrowding and multiple-coding, the defence against which is cool indifference.

Indifference is merely the 'flight' end of the so-called 'fight or flight' response. It is the decathexis of the frenzied world, the schizoid withdrawal into a bubble of the educated, but disaffected masses. The 'fight' end appears occasionally when a lone gunman shoots at random, when maddening cries in his head spill over, not against his own body (autoimmune disease) but against the other, not as an enemy, but one whose *indifference* kills him. Each of us mentally has become a lone gunman irritated by everything but at the same time agreeing to everything and passionate about nothing. We include the other in our Imaginary (all progressive ideas of tolerance, etc.), while excluding and murdering him in the Real. Even the laws of physics are subtly changing. At one time you could count on the forces of repulsion and attraction (ambivalence). Now, increasingly, repulsion is the rule. *Opposites repel.*

Violent Effects

We have stressed the *totallising ascendancy* of the media-image and its associated mass autonomous functions, as the privileged means of representation — the creation of the world. If the symbol (representation) is the murder of the thing, how much more is the *mediated*-real the hidden *violence* of late capitalism? Reality has become a borderline concept; what is real is now open to serious doubt. Reality has become one of the 'disappeared', taken-out at night by agents, tied up, tortured, shot and buried in an unmarked grave.[6] As the trail grows fainter, the will to resist weakens. The real cannot survive under the immense burden of meaning and visibility that it is expected to yield.

If it were possible to see our own face in reality, it would cause madness, since we would no longer have any mystery for ourselves. We would be annihilated by transparency. Notwithstanding, we are all the more caught in and seduced by the mirror and its image. The paradox of psychoanalysis is that we must look at ourselves but *not* be found, lest we too become one of the disappeared. The secret here is that the object which *appears* has always already disappeared. In our cultural therapeutic moment, reality is jump-started: we are *forced* to see more and more, forced to believe, forced to know. The (news) stories that are told, on the spot reports, event analysis, the copious meanings found and looked for everywhere, shore up a world, mental equilibrium depends on it. The Promethean dare to technologically realise the world and criminally perfect it, is also the climax of technological nihilism and wholesale loss.

Our appetite to *see* knows no bounds, homing in on every disaster with our bad conscience and humanitarian aid. We will even fit out missiles with their own nose-cone cameras to penetrate to the heart of the Real in the act of obliteration (in slow motion, in replay), *on screen, to see everything.*[7] The terrifying image of the Twin Towers was relayed instantaneously around the world and then has been reproduced endlessly since in spin-off stories, where the voyeuristic impulse is hidden under the legitimating guise of human interest.

At the endoscopic level: tubes, mucosa, every orifice penetrated, secretions traced to the obscene moment of fertilisation itself. Recently, a doctor dissects a dead body on stage, 'to demystify death, the last great taboo'. At the macroscopic level, the scopic field around the earth (the scoposphere complete with satellites that can see down to a few centimetres) and to the furthest reaches of the universe.

Then, we must see *ourselves* helping all those victims, those Others who are the remaindered of representations. These are the *unnamed* peasants, the poor, driven from their homes in carts and tractors by the violence of representation, of sign systems, ideologies backed as always by the cynical escalation of the global free-market in arms. The violent effects of the burgeoning hyperreal are everywhere. What is excluded is none other than life itself, in its *substantial* being, which is cut through, exploded by the terrorism of the sign.[8]

Similarly, therapy culture, having promoted the atomising liberation of civic society is moved to counsel the huge deposits of casualties that are the guarantee of its future. We are only starting. Hypocrisy must be exposed at every level: in institutions (via group therapy); between people (via relationship counselling); in the mind (via psychotherapy); the hypocrisies within the body (via bio-energeticists); within the cell (via genetic modification). There is nowhere to hide from the shining light (example to us all!) of therapy ideology.[9] It will come as no surprise to see the piety and humility of all the caring services and media who now profit in so many publicly financed and privately financed ways by picking up the evacuated pieces, the body pieces, as it were, of the war-torn site of the social.[10]

And it *is* a war. As the permafrost of the Cold War has given way to global warming by therapeutic processes, we might be lulled into thinking that the rage of the universe, as singularly concentrated in nuclear armaments, has evaporated in the magically warm glow of what people still believe will come: the sentimental integral order. The point here is that therapy, all the caring corporations and institutions that embody therapeutic values are merely a screen, or, better still, a net which serves as a reaction formation. In short, therapy *is* the nuclear option: everything else has been blown away. As Virilio reminds us, interactivity may yet be as dangerous as radioactivity. We need no reminding that our nets and webs (of care) had military origins and that IBM's first computing machines were used to count the victims of the Holocaust. Right now, the much celebrated freedom of networking (yes, outside of authoritarian controls!) only serves to mask the net's own total surveillance possibilities that are increasing exponentially. Our worlds are becoming remorselessly transparent.

Liberal v Radical

Jameson proposes our new historically original dilemma,

> . . . that involves our insertion as individual subjects into a multidimensional set of radically discontinuous realities, whose frames range from the still-surviving spaces of bourgeois private life all the way to the unimaginable decentring of global capital itself (Jameson, 1991, p. 413).

If those still surviving spaces (transitional, private, solitary, psychoanalytic) are shrinking fast, will there indeed come a time when no one will *remember* what they stood for?

Here is an important distinction between a liberal and a radical perspective on postmodernism. The liberal position, when indeed it considers the 'system', does not consider it 'total' in the way that we have been stressing. It can be ameliorated, regulated, patched-up — from this centred position of bourgeois privacy, freedom and objectivity. Moreover, we are now in a position to be truly free to use the new opportunities offered by information technology. As liberal autonomous subjects in a democracy, we have everything — access to every sign, commodity, service. We have more wealth than at any other time. Living standards have risen more than threefold in the last fifty years and for the first time, there are unprecedented opportunities, especially for the young and (middle-class) women.

All liberal democracies share the ideology of care and human rights. In this frame, it is only a matter of time before (re)-education, especially in the form of mass therapy, finally percolates down to the masses so that everyone will respect everyone else, nobody's rights will be infringed. This insistent positivity is a utopian leftover from high modernist notions of planned and scientifically run economies, cities and societies. Reason, spread by education for choice and consumption, underpins liberal morality. The Left believes in equal rights for all minorities. The Right believes in the free market. Both operate as a reasonable cover and a screen that enables ruthless exploitation to go on unhindered. For inatance, it is reliably estimated that there are more slaves in the world than at the time of the abolition of slavery during the mid-19th Century. The arrival of McDonalds in Moscow marked the beginning of the virulent colonisation of the East, and the creation, within a few years, of dereliction on a scale never seen before and the so-called criminal superstates.[11] This was the great *humiliation* of communism, not by a Great Idea (the liberal tradition), but by the free-play of the Market.

With the evaporation of the old Left, a bland consensus exists within the liberal establishment (the Third Way) which is ever more blind to the Real. Only layers of security and electronic gadgetry, secret service agents, media minders, scriptwriters, spin-doctors, make-up people, and so on, unheard of only a few decades ago, forming a total ecosystem, perpetuates itself in the wider media culture, severed from, talking against, talking down another reality.

On the phone to some large or small corporation, and immediately, we are on first name terms — time, distance, otherness erased. Leaving the shopping precinct, there is a sign which thanks us *personally* for shopping here. The till receipt tells me who served me, the date, the hour and the minute, at which I paid — all uselessly caring. I am thanked for flying on this airline, told that this packaging is kind to the environment, this corporation is ethically committed. Thank you for banking, parking, choosing us. Thank you for your call, all our lines are busy at present . . . Please know that we really value your custom . . . Thank you for waiting. Thank you for bringing this to our attention. Thank you for sharing your pain with us. And so on. Yet everyone knows: *real* courtesy no longer exists. It has been replaced by all the technical *signs* of courtesy. Liberalism no longer exists: it has disappeared into the mass commercialisation of 'freedom'.

Post-Fordist management is flexible, open, anti-authoritarian, non-hierarchical, young and participatory. The ideology of transparency and openness enables the culture to preserve its financial, professional and educated elites (ever more so), while espousing and expertly promoting specifically *anti*-elitist leftist democratic values. The signs of status are consumed everywhere, and 'losing' bears a very heavy sense of *visible* personal failure coerced as we are into the *same* consumer game in which the goals have recently become infinitely extended in terms of wealth and power.[12] Very few of us are *not* losers because the current imaginary of aspirations knows *no* limits. We bear a much heavier sense of failure and futility, than in the days when real oppression and authority were both more evident and unjustifiable. On the contrary, as this new game[13] is promoted as fun, easy and democratic, the sense of losing is multiply acute — being seen to fail on the one hand, at a game you *should have been able to play*, on the other, realising that you have no one to blame but yourself. Resentment is impossible because that only confirms your inferior, isolated status as unwilling or unable to play the game and enjoy it. After all, the game is enjoyment, and you apparently can't enjoy yourself! You have to bear the shame alone, as your fellow consumers *appear*, like stars in the universe, to be travelling at higher and higher speeds away from you. Furthermore, transparency and responsibility will mean that failure will stare at you continuously from every screen and minitor, from every commercial.

The success of liberal democracies has meant that the new elites of the system have arisen more meritocratically than heretofore. They are the first rationally created elites. Unlike older ones they feel they can justify their ascendancy position. However, older elites felt some obligation to those they oppressed. The new elites have abandoned this vestige of civility. Ironically, they would resent the term 'elite' as applied to them, indicating that their natural political sympathies would still be with the left and equality. However, they can by-pass all the *public* services. Private education means their children do not have to go to decaying inner-city schools. Ninety per cent of the top 200 British schools are private. Corporate, or group private health schemes short-circuit long waiting lists in public hospitals; private pensions ensure a comfortable old age; private security supplements the failure of public crime prevention. They can selectively buy their own entertainment, and when the public transport system has become chaotic, they can pay for their four wheel drives, for toll roads, air transport for several holidays a year and so on. Elitism or wealth is not wrong per se, but these 'winners' sever the links, of

obligations and duties at the local and community level in prefer-
ence to networking *internationally* and globally in the field of work
and leisure. These elites include brokers, bankers, developers, engi-
neers, consultants of all types, scientists, doctors, therapists, university professors, publishers, editors, media people, journalists,
executives and artists. For these liberals, the system works and they
play it for all they are worth.

The *radical* position, on the other hand, envisages the absolute con-
striction of the total system of consumption, now unleashed without
interruption to feed on everything without restraint. A system of
predation in which we are situated unable to muster the moral
resources to imagine a future. This is what Bahro following Lewis
Mumford calls the 'megamachine'. He says: 'Today we are forced to
speak apocalyptically, not because of culture pessimism, but
because this destructive side is gaining the upper hand . . . that in the
set of rules guiding the evolution of our species, death has made its
home' (Bahro, 1994, p. 19).

From this perspective, the system is like a vast game that you must
play hard and enjoy. Enjoyment is the ruse of the system to free-up
the 'happy consciousness' eager for aggressive hyper-consumption.
So it is no accident that sport is taken more seriously by more people
than virtually any other activity. Sport has left the political field
decathected and empty. The consumption of sport and the sport of
consumption is the sum total of a vast tautological system of 'scoring', turning around the one *phallic* exchange standard. One Irish
Men's magazine exhorts its readers to 'work hard, play hard and
stay hard!' The language of the ghetto extends to the middle classes
and corporation executives alike, always screwing, scoring, shaft-
ing, getting it up, getting it in, coming on, pulling it off, everywhere
the rhetoric of aggressive phallocracy. The game is above all a phallic
game, in which you either have it, want it, or you go for it. The worst
state is to be without it. And our freedom is the liberation from any
constraint in respect of making it, no holes barred.

Freedom carries the greatest weight of the Good in liberal democracies and therapy is right there to promote freedom and to overcome any remaining inhibitions and obstacles in respect of
enjoyment. Freedom is the vertigo of the diffusion of loyalty and the
catastrophic losses of ordinary loves. We have become like Bowlby's
institutionalised children, who, having cried out for their absent
mothers to the point of exhaustion and finally despair, permanently
exclude people in favour of toys and objects. The average supermarket
carries between twenty and thirty thousand different products or
goods. All these goods must add up! All these goods must fill up,

must symbolise, must stand in for, *the absolute withdrawal of the Other*. Freedom is flooding the world with its love substitutes.[14]

Nothing can separate us from the love of the universal code to which we are assigned, into which we are 'thrown', by the autonomous language of capitalism, assigned to this particular real in the twenty-first century to the point of total permeability. Paralysis and inertia born of apathy and boredom form the backdrop, against which we can only erect and play our 'willy games.'[15] Unconscious desire, at one time a privileged notion, invented and preserved for a time by psychoanalysis, a hidden subversive force, is caught by the beautiful logic of the Free World. The unconscious depended on repression — the sequestration of signifiers, reserves of hidden strength and uncolonised desire. Currently there is controlled *decompression* — the programmed release of moral pressure leading to a free and generalised cooling and contraction.

The radical position asserts that capitalism is now part of a whole process of complexification, which ultimately proceeds *without us*. The human race is, so to speak, 'pulled forward' by this vast process without possessing the slightest means for mastering it. According to Lyotard, for instance,

> The electronic and information network spread over the earth gives rise to a global capacity for memorising which must be estimated at the cosmic scale. . . . The paradox implied by this memory resides in the fact that in the last analysis it is *nobody's memory* (Lyotard, 1988a, p. 68).

Therefore, the real *user* of language is not the human mind *qua* human, but complexity in movement, of which *our* mind, *our* cherished activity (indeed interactivity), *our* free choices are only ever a mere support for this system. Lyotard says that we are at the point of, 'the infinite realisation of the sciences, technologies and capitalism', and the production of the '*too beautiful*' (p. 122). This, 'too', signifies that we are marginal to the product, surplus to requirements! It is beyond us. We are only needed for the process of consumption. There is no longer a possibility of an *originary* giving and receiving (termed 'passibility'[16] by Lyotard), because the commodified is already approaching perfection itself. All that is left is an infinite passivity of a *simulated* giving and receiving, communication, the robotic response, no more than the exchange of a virtual infinity of the Same.

Therapy refutes any notion of an *exterior* to the system where life might still be found. Therapy is the system and the system is therapeutic. Therapy oils the wheels of the system of free-floating lifestyles. If, for instance, you cannot grasp, speak, or represent yourself, then you don't exist. *You are exterior. You are silence.* You have the freedom to say what you want! Go for it! But I cannot speak,

I cannot speak the unspeakable exteriority of the therapeutic games you want me to play. I must be the *dis*-ease of the system. This is no counter-game of not speaking, a stubborn refusal to dialogue, the other side of the same, but the alterity of the unconscious itself. I cannot speak my life. I cannot come-out in this way. Otherness is unspeakable. Otherness tears through speech, but cannot be encompassed. Only on *this* (non-)basis can we 'meet', the basis of an irredeemable *separation* in which you and I will never know each other. However, therapy rests on the inhuman total light of the system, that knows no shadows.

The subject is always separated, alienated *from* his work, his labour, what he produces. Nowhere is this more true than when the work is *oneself*, in therapy, the production of a better person. Here, the finished 'product' is the beginning of the consumption of the self and other, the oiling of the system of our current state of the inhuman exchange.

Effraction

Therapy is the system and the system is ever more sophisticatedly complete in its totallising function, in that it mops up all potential opposition, while democratically providing ample location for difference. How can there ever be a breakthrough or a breakout? Why should we even want one? In fact, to speak as we have done throughout about the code, the system of violence masquerading as care, its totality, its transcendent success, risks a serious negative diagnosis by that same system. We can no longer turn to therapists for help, as they are at the very heart of the thought process of the system! Instead, we must invoke our shadowy dissidents. Put the system on trial. Speak of crimes against humanity. Expose it where we can.

For Baudrillard, for instance, what is immanent to the system, what haunts it, is 'Symbolic Exchange' (Baudillard, 1976) which he derives from Marcel Mauss's celebrated analysis of gift exchange.[17] Baudrillard's interest in Mauss was to underpin his interest in symbolic exchange, that is in the inevitable reciprocity and equivalence of life and death, reversibility, evasion of all controls, chaos theory, consumption without end, agonistic relations, the play of challenge, the duel and seduction. In all these, the semiocratic order of the code is subverted from within by the counter-logic of the symbolic or initiatory (dis)orders. He uses the term 'effraction' to designate these catastrophic effects that arise from the operation of the system itself.

Symbolic exchange cannot be barred (by the Lacanian bar), there is no sense of a dialectical 'return of the repressed', because the symbolic knows no repression; it has no sign and is of no value, but criminally subverts all values to do with rationality, need, differentiation and the law. Its power is not phallic and accumulative; rather, the power of many absences — the secret, the ruse, the counter-gift, singularly unexpected! The only bar that Baudrillard recognises is not the bar between signifier and signified, but is the bar of radical exclusion, of Otherness.

As Genosko points out,

> Baudrillard does not and cannot explain how communication could take place if encoding or decoding did not occur between persons. Instead what he focuses on is the obligation (which 'replaces' the code — understood as cold, remote and digital) to give and receive *between* persons in the absence of their abstract separation and togetherness (Gonosko, 1994, p. 36).

The implication is that there is something unseen that slips beyond and within the univocality/polyvocality of the code, which is annulled by it and thereby retains its secret parallel life which has to do with some lost real of the social. Seize it 'therapeutically' and you're done for. The danger is in *talking* about it!

Baudrillard refuses to get into a rant about the code. He continuously resists the twin temptations of the fall into nothingness on the one hand and the creation of a strong counter-theory on the other — producing a moralistic critique or denunciation which only buttresses the same system it critiques. His deconstructive turn is at once tactical, cunning, fluid and ironic. To demonstrate the indifferent nihilism of the code and its supra-authority, Baudrillard is the victim, and places himself of necessity, as victim of what Lyotard refers to as a Differend.

There is a differend when a conflict between two parties cannot be resolved or judged fairly due to the lack of a rule of judgement which applies *equally* to both parties. The victim is one who has suffered a wrong yet lacks any means with which to prove his case. Lyotard's example is with Marxist theory itself, which

> thus presented itself not as *one* party in a suit, but as judge, as the science in possession of objectivity, thereby placing the other in the position of stupor or stupidity . . . incapable of making itself understood, unless it borrowed the dominant idiom — that is, unless it betrayed itself (Lyotard, 1988b, p. 61).

Freud had his own version of the differend. You could not criticise psychoanalysis unless you had been analysed, in which case, you would not want to. Similarly, it is impossible to criticise a system that therapeutically absorbs all dissent. Therefore, Baudrillard's writing is agonistic and sacrificial, doubling itself, annulling and then self annulling, giving the gift of itself and the counter-gift of its own disappearance.

Baudrillard's irony plays on the hegemony of the code, always and everywhere undercut by its own radically excluded (il)logic. That is, the linear and accumulative strategy of capitalism, and, in the rhetoric of human resources, 'personal growth', set against reversibility and the abundant wastage of symbolic exchange. The cycle of exchange never ends. However, as contemporary capitalism moves to annihilate all reference to utility, reality and value, it comes ever closer to the orgy of the potlatch immanent to the system itself. The recycling effect that the code generates, feeding on itself (the consumption of consumption), in the absence of any real, risks abolishing its own determinacy, its own ends. It is about to achieve weightlessness.

Baudrillard does not pit a primitive mystical fatalism of the potlatch against the global system as if to overturn it with yet another system, but rather mobilises those fatal forces within the system itself, amplifying the chaotic techno-simulations until they topple over into irreconcilability. As the Real has already passed over into the illusion, one has to recognise the reality of the illusion and play upon the power it exerts. Baudrillard concludes: 'He [man] cannot be accused of a superior egoism. He is sacrificing himself, as a species, *to an unknown experimental fate*' (Baudrillard, 1992, p. 83).

Radical Psychoanalysis

Michel Henry in his rigorous work, *The Genealogy of Psychoanalysis*, throws down a challenge, a critique, to contemporary psychoanalysis, analogous to Baudrillard's 'signs must burn'. Psychoanalysis, by privileging representations, whether conscious or unconscious, fails to make the crucial distinction between representation and its radical Other, namely, *affectivity*. The Freudian concept of the unconscious has two fundamentally different meanings: the first pertaining to representations (present to consciousness or not), the second, to affects and affectivity or drive derivatives — more generally: part of the continuous upwelling of life itself and its inevitably *hidden* movement towards force and action in the world. Therefore, our current focus on texts, codes, signifiers, etc., obscures this second meaning of the unconscious: life's unconsciousness *of* itself, what Henry calls, life's auto-affection, its freedom and self immanence.

Henry rails against,: '[t]he denaturation of psychoanalysis by linguistics. . . . In all seriousness, people can now say that the unconscious is structured like a language' (Henry, 1985, p. 292). He prefers the formula: the unconscious is unstructured like an affect. Life is disturbance, disequilibrium, proximity, suffering — more nonsense than sense. It cannot be pressed or subjugated to meanings; rather the reverse, the current proliferation of the universal code becomes nihilistic, inspiring terror. The *power* that produces the dream, the joke, the slip, the commercial product, etc., is not the power of representational consciousness or of the universal code, but purely an excess. This power opens onto representation's wholly Other. The Freudian unconscious, ceasing to be merely the formal negation of the quality 'consciousness', takes on a life of its own, aiming at the very possibility of action — force, energy, power, madness, ultimately the death drive and Symbolic Exchange.

At the heart of neurotic suffering is an inability to tolerate the damming-up of libidinal tension which is equivalent to (an excess of) life itself. All the subject wants to do is to employ the libido, spend it to reduce its energy level, leading to self-suppression via the code or indeed a death-like quiescence of gratification. Likewise, psychoanalysis, with its current focus on language, shows all the signs of being afraid of life. As Henry says: 'Freudianism accounts for life only to liquidate it' (p. 313). The ultimate point to which the subject might go in this regard is the death drive and Nirvana itself, re- establishing the inertia inherent in inorganic life. 'Psychoanalysis is the soul of a world without soul, the spirit of a world without spirit' (p. 7).

What Henry is (re)claiming for a radical psychoanalysis is the immediacy of the Real as irrecuperably closer to us than the equivocations of language and the repressive distractions and displacements of the code. Language cannot contain the anarchic plot, which is elicited by silence, by the disorganising effects of free association, by 'unspeaking' (deparole), by the evolving ambivalent passions of transference and countertransference. A balance of forces emerges, a *hidden* order of ruse, challenge, game, suggestion, seduction, simulation, where each is hostage to the other: over-exposed, out of phase, out of sync, at risk — *sub-jectum*.

As Levinas says, solidarity *precedes* communication. In our pre-originary susceptibility, before the first, I am another. The urgent question is: does communication *preclude* solidarity? Once involved in therapeutic consumption, there is an inevitable and irretrievable kinetic effect, a gradual heating driving the molecules faster and faster and further and further apart, until we reach the current state of virtual vapourisation and dissociation. 'To catch the secret of our being', Henry asserts, '[w]e must hack back through a forest of symbols to find the great paths along which drives have tried to discharge themselves and by which life has tried to be rid of itself . . . exploded and dispersed across the ek-stasis of time' (pp. 325–6). Against the notion of a system, or, any kind of Idealism, Henry pits *auto*-affirmation, hyperpower, silence, immanance, presence and suffering.[18] But, fortunately, there is in fact no 'catching', as each subject is an ungraspable singularity, refusing registration and exposition while appearing to acquiesce (Winnicott's false self), playing the speech games and the castration games of loss and the 'depressive position', all these apologies for living, while *being disturbance* (the imprisonment of which is neurosis), while being obsessed, being moved, to the point of outpouring . . .

Not health, or wealth, but *stealth*, ours can only be a stealth system.

Malaise

Our culture is a national health system: everything must be healthy and clinics proliferate — political clinics, financial, sports, sexual, even health clinics. Everything is clinical. Clinical well-being, antisepsis, is at the heart of therapy culture. Hospitality, the unconditional welcoming of the other soul, has been replaced by its clinical equivalent, the hospital — the commercial 'welcome' of the technical object. We are working flat out to avoid death.

From the point of view of the soul, psychiatry is narcoterrorism while counselling and therapy is *Jihad*, an ideological struggle, the war of the mother, the mother of all wars. As subjects, we are bound over to keep the peace and to live with both of these sanitary ideologies. Holy war has been declared on the Real and the Real has given way to its perfected clinical image. The subject, part of that real, no longer exists. It too has disappeared hoping that nothing real will ever happen to it. Playing along is as much as it can manage. Playing dead while displaying all the vital signs, putting in an occasional appearance (mostly to check, receive or relay a message).

In the midst of rapid and continuous change, revolution, the holy wars of our therapists, the recreational, criminal or medical fight for control of our moods, the hidden murder of the Real, the collective process of mourning cannot take place. When so much is being lost so quickly, *mourning* cannot take place and permanent melancholia ensues. Depression is endemic in the West. When so much is being gained so quickly, mourning is impossible. As spending itself becomes unreal, it is like a never-ending grieving process, a dying that will never end.

In the normal process of mourning, Freud states:

> Reality-testing has shown that the loved object no longer exists, and it proceeds to demand that all libido shall be withdrawn from its attachments to that object. This demand arouses considerable opposition . . . [which] can be so intense that a turning away from reality takes place and clinging to the object through the medium of a hallucinatory wishful psychosis.

Normally, reality gains the upper hand and, 'Each single one of the memories and expectations in which the libido is bound to the object is brought up and hypercathected, and detachment of the

libido is accomplished in respect of it' (Freud, 1917, p. 245). This cannot now happen. The loved object of the Real has disappeared. Fearing the actual death of the Real, but hoping against hope for its
miraculous survival somewhere in the ruins, the ritualistic process
of mourning does not happen. Instead, as we have stressed all along,
we are stuck fast at the hypercathexis stage of the non-process,
libidinising, thematising, hallucinating, every lost repetitious nostalgic detail of the Real.

In the case of melancholia, Freud tells us, there is some loss of an
ideal kind often due to some hurt, separation or end of a loving relationship. Freud speaks of this as an unconscious loss, with the result
that there is not the normal withdrawal of libido from this loved
object and the displacement of it onto a new one but that,

> it was withdrawn into the ego . . . ser[ving] to establish an identifica-
> tion of the ego with the abandoned object. Thus the shadow of the
> object fell upon the ego, and the latter could henceforth be judged by
> a special agency, as though it were an object, the forsaken object
> (p. 249).

Unable to find the Real to mourn, we have withdrawn into ourselves
and our apartments, *shadowed* by the Real that follows, that mocks,
that flickers at us from the mirror of every screen. We become hopelessly identified with our own abandonment, locked in, alone and
judged by that 'special agency' Freud designates as the ego ideal,
which signals the depressed and shameful abandonment of all ideals.

Ambivalence to the world was normal, but when the world aban-
dons us, with no real to test, ambivalence regresses, as Freud suggests, to the most primitive oral sadism. The lost world hates and
condemns humanity to morbid addictive cravings, on the increase
everywhere — the manic flight from the devastated real, which
responds malignly to produce perfected hallucinations of itself as a
revenge for it own disappearance. No chance of reparation either.
No entry into the depressive position, as there is nothing to repair
and nothing to feel guilty about.

Lacan emphasised that language creates a void, represented by
the vaunted spaces of ancient architecture, the empty enclosure of
the vase, the ring of torus and its internal dimension, the absent
sacred space of the Thing — all outlining the gravitational pull of
loss as a strange attractor. However, unable to conceive of loss, we go
panic-buying, which becomes an exponential provision and accumulation of metonymical objects. We have *become* loss: loss inhabits
us, as a lost cause. We have been given up on, left to wander alone in
the cosmos!

At the end of her book, *Powers of Horror*, Kristeva writes of the
abyss of abjection which, 'is the other facet of religious, moral, and

ideological codes on which rest the sleep of individuals and the breathing spells of societies' (Kristeva, 1980, p. 209). Such codes purify and repress the abject. With these codes destroyed, torn up, ridiculed and replaced by their ecstatic and sacrificial forms, the pot-latch, the consumption of consumption, no individual can sleep and no society can breathe.

The question posed by this book is whether counselling, therapy culture or the whole apparatus of universal care is equal to these atomisations. Having thoughtlessly helped to precipitate them and having forsworn any pretence at depth (we're pleased to announce that we are only in the business of managing change) can they do any more than put a very brave face on things, while exploiting the ruins? And is psychoanalysis any more than just a tiny enclave increasingly irrelevant in the new emotional world order? Perhaps so, particularly as it has carelessly made itself part of it. Yet, as Kristeva claims: '[T]he analyst, since he interprets, is probably among the rare contemporary witnesses to our dancing on a volcano allow[ing] the most deeply buried logic of our anguish and hatred to burst out' (pp. 209–10).

This may be granting the analyst too much (authority) particularly as he/she long ago forswore clarity and any metaperspective. Preoccupied with the clinic and the academy, and engaged like everyone in endless deferral, displacement and appeasement, the field is left wide open to cranks of all persuasions who offer an alchemy for the horror.

The 20th Century avant-garde announced the triumphant end of everything, of the alleged separatist, elitist, masculinist notions of the Protestant bourgeoisie, the end of imperialistic models in all forms. Postmodernity marks the so-called 'return' to oriental wisdom, multiculturalism, to Woman, a new ethic of pluralist assent and care, One world, the earth as a therapeutic organism (Gaia), one universe (with us in mind from the beginning!), a break with anthropocentrism, a break with objectivity for new immersions in subjectivity, networking, new theologies, and so on and on. In the last few decades, there has been a virtual explosion of new ecstatic forms, of therapeutic-magico-religious rituals with a celebratory emphasis on the paranormal, the irrational, the ecological, the psychotropic — all in delirious flight and promiscuity. No longer circling the void (as in the torus), but hurtling away. Fighting is done with. Our adrenalin rush comes, not with adversarial conflict and Law enforcement, but with flight into everything via mutual arousal and connectedness. Whatever you're into; whatever turns you on, the flight into *jouissance*.

Everywhere the break from all the old values of domination, logico-positivism, mastery, distance, brutality, into the organic, the whole, in touch with 'the dance' of the atoms and molecules. The break from the glacial cold of the old Newtonian universe and the turn toward the warmth of the *feminine*, the endless encirclement, caress and virtually unlimited amniotic nutrition. Here, everything joins up and communicates via networks and superconductivity: instantaneous call up and back-up; the feminine is availability *without limit*.

However, set against this therapeutic ease and accessibility, are the viral forms and their multiplication. Against holism and sentimental forms, new forms of virulent scientific separatist imperialisms have been developing — molecular technologies, nanotechnology and genetic engineering. Behind the holistic rhetoric, the jungles are been raided for our last chance to exploit rare species for exotic new drugs before the slow tide of the most recent mass extinction takes these rare species with them. The new vogue for transgenic species surely represents a new obscene order of omnipotent manipulation. Up until about 20 years ago, the genetic *integrity* of species was sacrosanct. Now, this fundamental barrier has been broken as if to make a joke of the sovereignty of genomes: soil bacteria producing insulin; plants resistant to herbicides; animals promoting their own super-growth; giant salmon; designer hybrids; crops that produce their 'own' insecticides; mice with ears on their backs; spare embryos[19] for genomics research at the aptly named Wellcome Institute. The new Right advanced deregulation in economics. A more extreme position is deregulation in genomics, a free market of genes, gene lay-off, the privatisation and the patenting of genes.[20] More broadly, this is de-generation, the loss of what constitutes a genus. It is also the most extreme end of the whole spectrum of therapeutic intrusiveness.

In instances like these, the therapeutic placates its own death drive, as if advanced technologies had gotten fed up with the whole enlightenment project of caring and human advancement, and turned demonic, secretly enjoying the prospect of new exotic extinctions and the global experiment.[21]

Caught in the zero gravity of the postmodern, we have tried to capture the virulence of the disappearance of the Real, the new weightlessness of thinking, of groundless therapeutics, where there is no 'truth' to uncover behind the veil of appearances. The unreal is what is consumed and promoted and what we have left to enjoy is truly unreal!

There is a backdrop here, namely, the half-century old threat of nuclear conflagration, mutual deterrence and the perpetual darkness of a nuclear winter. Only the protective illusory shield of therapy and total care can hide and deter, the apocalypse. The Internet, which has enabled the rapid globalisation of therapeutic logic, began as a net for American strategic defense. It now presides over our very own *electronic* intimacy and transparency, the digital veil that at every site marks the disappearence of the other and a loss too great to record, to be measured increasingly on a global scale.

Notes

1. One can detect in Freud's work two contradictory currents. Freud one: the revelation of the unconscious, and the decentring of the ego, on the one hand in works likes the *Studies in Hysteria* (1893–5), *The Interpretation of Dreams* (1900), *Jokes and their Relation to the Unconscious* (1905), *The Psychopathology of Everyday Life* (1901). As against, Freud two: the commitment to strengthen the ego against those same forces, in for instance, *The Ego and the Id* (1923) and *Inhibitions, Symptoms and Anxiety* (1926).

2. Every deviant form of sexual activity is available to download. Is this simply regression to powerful violent archaic traces of pre-Oedipal phantasies, described by Melanie Klein, deep in the unconscious of all of us? Or, is pornography merely an excrescence of the current state of free-play in the unregulated market which psychoanalysis tells us must always drive beyond the reality principle.

3. Even experimental science, once believed for its objectivity, is now widely distrusted. Pronounce that a certain food is safe to eat and everyone asks: who is funding them? Science becomes ideologically framed.

4. Recently Baudrillard (2002) referred to the World Trade Center collapse as an image of the West's suicide.

5. Compared to the Real of war, the post-war economic boom coming as it did after the privations of war, undoubtedly welcome, ushered a golden age of unprecedented material increase, but also created the rise of a new psychopathology of everyday life: which soap powder gets clothes whitest? Colgate rings of confidence, etc.

6. The disappeared in Ireland. Provisional IRA informers during the 1970s and 1980s were shot and buried in unmarked graves. Many of the bodies have never been recovered in spite of intense efforts by the authorities during the Peace Process.

7. One press photographer reveals the lengths he went to, to get a picture of a burnt out train, bombed by accident by a NATO missile aiming at a bridge in the former Yugoslavia. What was important was to get the best picture of this little piece of the Real and to wire it to his newspaper ahead of the others so as to make the front page.

8. What was truly exemplary about the death of Diana in Paris was that she was being pursued by the media and that the fatal crash was but the last event in a long line of aggressive intrusions/invitations into her life. On the morning of her death there were physical attacks on the reporters and photographers who were trying to record the initial public grief. Then the focus shifted to other events around the crash, the intoxication of their driver, the British public's idealisation of her life, the distance of the Royal Family, etc. What is important here is that she was caught in/fixated in the imaginary, seduced by the imagery which proliferated to represent her life, from which she became increasingly absent until she disappeared completely while her image 'lives' on.

9. Immediately, it will be argued that therapy *allows* people to speak and represent themselves, in total contrast to the violent imposition of ideologies

on a passive population in a war situation. Yes, but, even before the client comes into the consulting room, he/she has signed up, allowed themselves to be assigned to a sign system with a world view which, in the micro-political field, I have been arguing throughout, has been *devastating* to a whole range of social institutions and relationships, not least the family, the church, police, etc. *So much the better*, say our therapists with some glee, let them collapse, change, reform, etc., thereby revealing immediately their ideological weaponry!

10. The Irish media, for instance, parade victim after victim of the new sentimental disorder in radio programmes detailing their misery (always called their story, first names, much sympathy) with gushing expressions of concern issuing from the bad consciences of the media stars whose raw material has been for three decades the destitute other, particularly of the inner cities. During these decades their friends in the political classes practised corruption on a wide scale, with a good conscience. Together, the ruling intelligentsia (the media and political class) prey upon dereliction — part of their moral and professional duty to inform and, above all, to help.

11. As part of a series of programmes to mark the end of the millennium, the BBC's John Simpson interviewed the head of Interpol, who acknowledged openly that world's criminal syndicates are beyond the reach of the international and national policing bodies.

12. Think of the moving scenes of all those East Germans streaming across the border into the West in 1989 — to search, not for the idea of freedom at last, but to buy consumer goods, as if all courageous opposition to the system over the previous seventy years, the gulags, the suffering for freedom, all dissidence, has come to this. And more than a decade later, they still feel the shame, resentment and nostalgia for being obliged by their West German fellow hyper-consumers to be their own victims of the discredited system. The shame of seduction; the shame of failure.

13. There is now no irony attached to the description of our new dispensation as 'a game' you play. Life is a game, easy, cool, fun; you should make it work for you, the young person will say. But, is there a hint of despair in this notion? It is impossible to take *anything* seriously anymore. Nothing can be approached except in the spirit of fun. Maths must be fun, philosophy must be fun. Enjoy. Enjoy.

14. Freedom, voted in a poll the key word that best describes the 20th Century, includes now increasing and unprecedented freedoms. Beyond the most trivial 'choices' about which coffee to buy, come so-called lifestyle choices. With all traditional norms torn up, and the grounds for making an informed choice based on deep knowledge of traditions and mores, shifting violently, one might expect that most choices will be detrimental and premature. To take one example, the decision of some couples not to have children. Perhaps — we dare only say perhaps these days, for fear of jeopardising this freedom — the couple might come too late to the realisation that they have not escaped their narcissistic privileging of themselves, the breaking-free of the 'I'. They have missed forever, the possibility of what Levinas calls 'resuming the thread of history'. This is not just the passing on of genes, but the continuation of identity in the other who is not me. For Levinas, it is 'fecundity' that saves us from *an anonymous infinity* (see Levinas, 1947, section 4c).

15. A comment made about in-fighting by the only woman member on the board of a large media company.

16. 'Passibility' is a key term in Lyotard's later work. It is the state of being seized by what has not been conceptually anticipated, the Other, or what Kant called the big X.

17. Here Mauss explains the universal custom of compulsory gift giving and receiving. It is not the content of the gift that matters but its obligatory reversible form — gift reciprocated by counter-gift. In its extreme form, Mauss describes the potlatch of native North Americans where gift exchange develops to an extreme, out of control, into an orgiastic destruction of goods, in symbolic affirmation of the social bond. The reciprocity principle in symbolic exchange does not aim at rational equivalence (as in *economic* exchange) but requires the counter-gift to be greater than the gift. Things can spiral out of control and ceremonial destruction of goods is assured, which is beneficial to the spirits. The word potlatch means to feed or consume (see Mauss, 1950, p. 6). 'The potlatch is an example of a total system of giving ... each gift is part of a system of reciprocity in which the honour of the giver and the recipient are engaged. It is a total system in that every item of status or spiritual or material possession is implicated for everyone in the whole community' ... (Douglas in Mauss, p. viii). Failure to reciprocate means loss of the competition for honour. Similarly, the sacrifice is a gift that compels the deity to make a return. The theory of the gift is a theory of human solidarity, in which everything must circulate between the generations, the gods, the living and the ancestors. Mauss says, it is much more than a juridical phenomenon: 'It is a religious, mythological, and Shamanist [phenomenon], since the chiefs who are involved represent and incarnate their ancestors and the gods, whose name they bear, whose dances they dance and whose spirits possess them' (*Ibid.*, p. 38). There are *three* obligations: to give, to receive and to reciprocate. Gifts literally demand to be given away and destroyed! The contrast with Utilitarianism and with Liberal thought generally could not be more obvious.

18. Clearly Henry is not advocating (1) any return to nature, or, (2) a narcissistic self-affirmation or self-empowerment much favoured by counsellors and therapists, or, (3) any biological essentialism or archaim. His argument does not posit some 'beyond' or 'before' of language, but points to the phenomeno-logical *proximity* of life in its self-giving. All else is in some sense a profanity.

19. There are 'tens of thousands of frozen embryos in Europe' which may become available for donation for stem cell research. These are the so-called spare embryos donated for research by patients undergoing in vitro fertilisation. (Report in *Nature* on the deliberations of the European Commission's European Group on Ethics in Science and New Technologies, *Nature, 408* p. 277, 2000).

20. Behold another sleight of hand. 'Deregulation' signifies freedom from artificial, bureaucratic government controls or red tape. But this is but another masquerade because deregulation in all areas signifies more freedom to control and exploit in ever more subtle ways. The brakes are taken off and every market is freed up. Therapy is deregulation and freedom from constraints, but in reality it is hedged about with all kinds of terms, conditions and protective disclaimers, protocols, procedures.

21. One theory about the *non*-appearance of visitors from advanced civilisations, the absence of 'signals' that might indicate other life out there, is that these civilisations have killed themselves when their technologies have reached a certain advanced state. There may be something fundamentally incompatible about advanced technology and the continuance of civilisation.

Bibliography

Amis, M. (1989) *London Fields*. London: Jonathan Cape.

Amis, M. (2002) *Koba the Dread*. London: Jonathan Cape.

Bahro, R. (1994) *Avoiding Social and Ecological Disaster*. London: Gateway Books.

Baudrillard, J. (1976) *Symbolic Exchange and Death*. Editions Gallimard. Trans. Iain Hamilton Grant. London: Sage. 1993.

Baudrillard, J. (1979) *Seduction*. Paris: Edition Galilée. Trans. B. Singer. Montreal: New World Perspectives. CultureText Series. 1990.

Baudrillard, J. (1983) *Fatal Strategies*. Paris: Editions Grasset. Trans. P. Beitchman and W. Niesluchowski. New York: Semiotext(e).

Baudrillard, J. (1980-85) *Cool Memories*. Paris: Editions Galilée. Trans. Chris Turner. London: Verso. 1990.

Baudrillard, J. (1990) *The Transparency of Evil*. Paris: Editions Galilée. Trans. James Benedict. London: Verso. 1993

Baudrillard, J. (1992) *The Illusion of the End*. Paris: Editions Galilée. Trans. Chris Turner. London: Polity Press. 1994.

Baudrillard, J. (2002) *The Spirit of Terrorism*. Paris: Edition Galilée. Trans. Chris Turner. London: Verso.

Bion, F. (Ed.) (1992). *W.R. Bion Cogitations*. London: Karnac.

Bion, W. (1965) *Transformations*. London: Heinnemann. Karnac. 1984.

Bion, W. (1970) *Attention and Interpretation*. London: Tavistock. Karnac. 1984.

Borch-Jacobsen, M. (1991) *Lacan. The Absolute Master*. Trans. D. Brick. California: Stanford University Press.

Chasseguet-Smirgil, J., Grunberger, B. (1976) *Freud or Reich? Psychoanalysis and Illusion*. Paris: Collection Les Abysses. Trans. Claire Pajaczkowska. London: Free Association Books. 1986.

Cooper, D. (1971) *The Death of the Family*. London: Allen Lane The Penguin Press.

Coupland, D. (1998) *Girlfriend in a Coma*. London: Flamingo.

Derrida, J. (1992) *The Gift of Death*. Paris: Transition. Trans. David Wills. Chicago and London: University of Chicago Press. 1995.

Derrida, J. (1996) *The Resistances of Psychoanalysis*. Paris: Editions Galilée. Trans. P. Kamuf, P-A. Brault, M. Naas. Stanford: Stanford University Press. 1998.

Dufourmantelle, A. and Derrida, J. (2000) *Of Hospitality*. Stanford, CA: Stanford University Press.

Eco, U. (1973) *Travels in Hyperreality*. Gruppo Editoriale Fabbri-Bompani, Sonzono, Etas. S.p.A. Picador. Trans. W. Weaver. New York: Harcourt Brace. 1990.

Evans, D. (1996) *An Introductory Dictionary of Lacanian Psychoanalysis*. London: Routledge.

Fenichel, O. (1946) *The Psychoanalytic Theory of the Neuroses*. London: Routledge Kegan Paul.

Freud, S. (1895) 'The Project for a Scientific Psychology'. In James Strachey, Ed., *The Standard Edition of the Complete Psychological Works of Sigmund Freud*, 24 volumes. Hogarth, 1953-73, Volume 1.

Freud, S. (1896) 'Draft K — The neuroses of defence' *S.E.* 1.

Freud, S. (1893-1895) *Studies in Hysteria. S.E.* 2.

Freud, S. (1894) 'The neuro-psychoses of defence.' *S.E.* 3.

Freud, S. (1899) 'Screen memories.' *S.E.* 3.

Freud, S. (1900) *The Interpretation of Dreams. S.E.* 4-5.

Freud, S. (1901) *The Psychopathology of Everyday Life. S.E.* 6.

Freud, S. (1905) *Jokes and their Relation to the Unconscious. S.E.* 8.

Freud, S. (1914) 'On narcissism: an introduction.' *S.E.* 14.

Freud, S. (1915) 'The unconscious.' *S.E.* 14.

Freud, S. (1917 [1915]) 'Mourning and melancholia.' *S.E.* 14.

Freud, S. (1920) *Beyond the Pleasure Principle. S.E.* 18.

Freud, S. (1923) *The Ego and the Id. S.E.* 19.

Freud, S. (1926) *Inhibitions Symptoms and Anxiety*. 1926. *S.E.* 20.

Freud, S. (1933a) 'The psychical dissection of the personality.' In *New Introductory Lectures on Psycho-Analysis. S.E.* 22.

Freud, S. (1933b) 'Femininity.' In *New Introductory Lectures on Psycho-Analysis. S.E.* 22.

Freud, S. (1937) 'Analysis terminable and interminable' *S.E.* 23.

Freud, S. (1939) *Moses and Monotheism. S.E.* 23.

Gardiner, M. 1971. *The Wolf-Man and Sigmund Freud*. London: Hogarth.

Gonosko, G. (1994). *Baudrillard and Signs*. London: Routledge.

Grotstein, J. (1978) 'Inner space: its dimensions and its co-ordinates.' *Int. J. Psycho-Anal*, 59: 55-61.

Hebdige, D. (1988) *Hiding in the Light*. London: Routledge.

Henry, M. (1985) *The Genealogy of Psychoanalysis*. Paris: Presses Universitaire de France. Trans. Douglas Brick. California: Stanford University Press. 1993.

Hitchens, P. (2003) *A Brief History of Crime*. London: Atlantic Books.

Hughes, R. (1993) *The Culture of Complaint*. New York: Oxford University Press.

Hussan, I. (1992) 'Pluralism in postmodern perspective.' In Jencks 1992.

Jameson, F. (1991) *Postmodernism, or the Cultural Logic of Late Capitalism.* London: Verso.

Jencks, C. (1992) *The Post-Modern Reader.* New York: St. Martin's Press. London: Academy Editions.

Khan, M. (1988) *When Spring Comes.* London: Chatto & Windus.

Klein, M. (1933) 'The early development of conscience in the child.' In M. Klein, *Love, Guilt and Reparation and Other Works 1921-1945.* London: Hogarth.

Klein, M. (1934) 'On criminality.' In M. Klein, *Love, Guilt and Reparation and Other Works 1921-1945. The Writing of Melanie Klein.* London: Hogarth. 1975.

Kristeva, J. (1980) *Powers of Horror.* Paris: Editions du Seuil. Trans. L. Roudiez. New York: Columbia University Press. 1982.

Kundera, M, (1991) *Immortality.* Trans. Peter Kussi. London: Faber and Faber.

Kundera, M. (2002) *Ignorance.* Trans. L. Asher. London: Faber and Faber.

Lacan, J. (1938) *Family Complexes in the Formation of the Individual.* Trans. C. Gallagher. School of Psychotherapy, St. Vincent's Hospital Dublin. (Unpublished).

Lacan, J. (1959-60) *Seminar VII. The Ethics of Psychoanalysis.* Paris: Edition du Seuil. Trans. Dennis Porter. London: Routledge. 1992.

Lacan, J. (1974) *Television.* Paris: Seuil. Trans. D. Hollier, R. Krauss, and A. Michelson, London: Norton.

Langton, C. (1997) *Artificial life.* See, for instance, http://www.webslave.dircon.co.uk/alife/intro.html

Laplanche, J. and Pontalis, B. (1974) *The Language of Psycho-Analysis.* London: Hogarth.

Levinas, E. (1947) *Time and the Other.* Grenoble-Paris: Arthaud. Trans. R. Cohen. U.S.: Duquesne University Press. 1987.

Levinas, E. (1981) *Otherwise than Being.* US: Kluwer Academic Publishers. Trans. A. Lingis. Pittsburgh: Duquesne University Press 1998.

Levinas, E. (2001) *Is it Righteous To Be.* Ed. Jill Robbins. California: Stanford University Press.

Loose, R. (2002) *The Subject of Addiction.* London: Karnac.

Lyotard, J-F. (1979) *The Postmodern Condition.* Manchester: Manchester University Press. 1984.

Lyotard, J-F. (1988a) *The Inhuman.* Paris: Editions Galilée. Trans. G. Bennington and R. Bowlby. Cambridge: Polity Press. 1991.

Lyotard, J-F. (1988b) *Peregrinations: Law, Form, Event.* New York: Columbia University Press.

Lyotard, J-F, (1993) *Postmodern Fables.* Paris: Editions Galilée. Trans. Georges van den Abbeele. University of Minnesota Press

MacIntyre, A. (1981) *After Virtue.* London: Duckworth.

McCourt, F. (1997) *Angela's Ashes. A Memoir of a Childhood.* London: Flamingo.

Marquez, G. Marcia (1998) *News of a kidnapping*. Trans. Edith Grossman. London: Penguin.

Masson, J. (1985) (Ed.) *The Complete Letters of Sigmund Freud to Wilhelm Fliess 1887-1904*. Cambridge, MA and London: Harvard University Press.

Mauss, M. (1950) *The Gift*. Presses Universitaires de France. Trans. W.D. Halls. London: Routledge. 1990.

Melman, C. 1980. 'Essay in clinical psychoanalysis: the alcoholic', in Schneiderman 1980.

Meltzer, D. (1978) *The Kleinian Development*. Clunie Press.

Neiderland, W. (1984) *The Schreber Case*. London: The Analytic Press.

Orwell, G. (1961) *Collected Essays*. London: Secker and Warburg.

Paz, O. (1986) 'The ghosts of religion.' *The Listener*. Vol. 115. (2956). 17/4/86.

Patocka, J. (1990) *Heretical Essays in the Philosophy of History*. Czech Academy of Science. Trans. Erazim Kohak. Illinois: Open Court. 1996.

Phillips, A. (1993) *On Kissing, Tickling and Being Bored*. London: Faber and Faber.

Poster, M. (1988) *Jean Baudrillard: Selected Writings*. London: Polity Press.

Rieff, P. (1966) *The Triumph of the Therapeutic*. London: Chatto and Windus. Harmondsworth: Penguin University Books. 1973.

Richards, B. (1994) *Disciplines of Delight: The Psychoanalysis of Popular Culture*. London: Free Association Books.

Richardson, W. (1998). 'The subject of ethics.' *The Letter* No. 14, pp. 3-26.

Showalter, E. (1997) *Hystories. Hysterical Epidemics and Modern Culture*. New York: Columbia University Press.

Schneiderman, S. (1980) *Returning to Freud. Clinical Psychoanalysis in the School of Lacan*. New Haven and London: Yale University Press.

Steiner, G. (1989) *Real Presences*. London: Faber and Faber.

Weatherill, R. (1994) *Cultural Collapse*. London: Free Association Books.

Weatherill, R. (1998) *The Sovereignty of Death.*. London: Rebus Press.

Weatherill, R. ed. (1999) *The Death Drive*. London: Rebus Press.

Winnicott, D. (1958) 'Psychoanalysis and the sense of guilt', in *The Maturational Processes and the Facilitating Environment*. London: Hogarth.

Winnicott, D. (1963) 'Communicating and not Communicating Leading to a Study of Certain Opposites.' In *The Maturational Processes and the Facilitating Environment*. Logarth.

Winnicott, D. (1987) *Home is Where We Start From*. London: Pelican Books.

Winnicott, D. (1988) *Human Nature*. Free Association Books.

Young, R. (1989) 'Post-Modernism and the subject.' London: *Free Associations, No.* 16.

Zizek, S. (1992) *Enjoy Your Symptom*. London: Routledge.

Zizek, S. (2000) *The Fragile Absolute*. London and New York: Verso.

SOCIETAS

essays in political and cultural criticism

Contemporary public debate has been impoverished by two competing trends. On the one hand the increasing commercialization of the media has meant that in-depth commentary has given way to the ten-second soundbite. On the other hand the explosion of scholarly knowledge has led to such a degree of specialization that academic discourse has ceased to be comprehensible. As a result writing on politics and culture tends to be either superficial or baffling.

This was not always so—especially for politics. The high point of the English political pamphlet was the seventeenth century, when a number of small printer-publishers responded to the political ferment of the age with an outpouring of widely-accessible pamphlets and tracts. Indeed Imprint Academic publishes a facsimile reprints under the banner 'The Rota'.

In recent years the tradition of the political pamphlet has declined—with most publishers rejecting anything under 100,000 words. The result is that many a good idea ends up drowning in a sea of verbosity. However the digital press makes it possible to re-create a more exciting age of publishing. *Societas* authors are all experts in their own field, but the essays are for a general audience. Each book can be read in an evening.

The books are available retail at the price of £8.95/$17.90 each, or on bi-monthly subscription for only £5.00/$10.50.Full details:

www.imprint-academic.com/societas

EDITORIAL ADVISORY BOARD

IMPRINT ACADEMIC, PO Box 200, Exeter, EX5 5YX, UK
Tel: (0)1392 841600   Fax: (0)1392 841478   sandra@imprint.co.uk